Burnout Is Not a Buzzword, It's a Diagnosis

An Educator's Survival Memoir in Sarcasm, Truth, and Grit

Burnout Is Not a Buzzword, It's a Diagnosis

An Educator's Survival Memoir in Sarcasm, Truth, and Grit

by

Dr. Dana Lebental, Ed.D.

BURNOUT IS NOT A BUZZWORD,

IT'S A DIAGNOSIS

ISBN: 979-8-9931164-0-2
First Edition, 2025
Published by Hall Pass Press
Pasadena, California
Cover Design: Dr. Dana Lebental
Illustrations: Dr. Dana Lebental using ChatGPT
Editor: Dr. Dana Lebental
Chief Red Pen Operator: Dead-Eye Dick
Formatting Wizardry: Joyce Beck
Library of Congress Control Number: 2025919703
Printed in the United States of America

Fan Mail—Not Just From My Mom

"This incredible book made me laugh, cry, and finally understand what teachers endure every day. It gave me new insight into what my daughter was going through as a teacher. A must-read for teachers, parents, and administrators."

— Miriam Lebental, Dana's Mother and #1 Fan

"Dana's story needs to be told, even though it breaks my heart. After more than three decades in education, I've seen both worlds: schools where teachers are supported and thriving — and schools where impossible challenges overshadow the joy of teaching. Dana captures the latter with honesty and urgency. We know how to make schools successful; it's time to make that happen everywhere."

— Valerie Saylor, Coordinator, New Teacher Development

"As a teacher of over two decades in a low-socioeconomic, urban community, I found Dana's book to be a deeply authentic and emotionally resonant portrayal of what it truly means to teach today. It doesn't sugarcoat: overcrowded classrooms, shifting policies, and the emotional toll are all laid bare. For those of us in the classroom, it feels like a mirror. For those outside—parents, policymakers, the public—it's a vital window into the profession's hidden labor and heartache. Reading it was validating, galvanizing, and, yes, laugh-out-loud funny in places I didn't expect. It made me want to retire early... but also reminded me why I stay."

— Tracy Williams, M.Ed., 20-Year Veteran Science Educator

Other Totally Real Reviews (Probably)

"It was so good I almost put down my phone. Almost."

— Former Student

"The only professional development I didn't sleep through."

— Anonymous Teacher, still bitter about PD bagels

"We thought we were helping. Turns out we were just providing Dana with material."

— Anonymous Policymaker, still wiping tears

"Finally, someone admits that yoga and scented candles don't cure burnout. My therapist thanks you."

— Fellow Burnout Survivor

Max-Head of Crisis Management (Unpaid)

DEDICATION

To the students who deserved more,

To the policymakers who called it "reform" while making it worse,

To my mom (yes, I know I get the summer "off," and no, that does not make it worth it),

To the fire alarms that made sure I never overcame my PTSD,

To Max — the only one who still sticks around through the chaos,

And finally, to me, Dr. Dana Lebental — for finding the grit and tenacity to turn burnout into a diagnosis, and survival into a story worth telling.

DISCLAIMER

Yes, the stories in this book are real. No, I didn't make them up — I'm not that creative.

The names and locations; however, have been changed. Why? Because I'd rather not get sued, fired, or side-eyed in the grocery store… or at the Castle.

The chaos, exhaustion, and absurdity? That part is 100% accurate.

Contents

INTRODUCTION: I NEED A DRINK. (AND MAYBE A LAWYER.)

Let's cut the crap: Education doesn't need "reform." It needs an exorcism. Everyone claims to love teachers, until we ask for a livable wage, a class size under 38, or a damn bathroom break. Then, we're told that we have the summers off.

You know what it's like being a teacher today? Imagine being locked in a room with 35 teenagers, one Chromebook charger, no air conditioning, a mouse that may or may not be dead behind the whiteboard and your email dinging every few minutes with "just checking in" messages from parents who've never once logged into the grade portal.

Plus: We're expected to stay calm, collected, and inspired while simultaneously dodging TikTok pranks, covering lunch duty, and being "voluntold" for another useless committee that will be renamed and repackaged next year with zero results.

Respect for teachers is alive and well, in inspirational Instagram quotes. "Back in My Day Historians," respected our martyrdom. "Future Lawsuit Enthusiasts" respect that we shut up and do it anyway. "Bureaucrats Without Borders" appreciate that we work for Target gift cards and Pinterest-level bulletin boards, as though this makes up for being screamed at by a 10th grader who hasn't eaten a vegetable since 2016.

So before you keep reading, "grab a drink?" What the hell, grab two ... vodka if you're a veteran, tequila if you're still pretending you'll make it to retirement.

This is not a love story. It's a survival manual written by someone who, in real life, had to inject Narcan into a foaming-at-the-mouth kid during 5th period while redirecting twenty-five other students to "stay focused on the mitosis lab." Welcome to teaching! Let's begin.

by Dr Dana

"I FOUND MY CALLING. TOO BAD IT WAS A PRANK CALL"

ALTERNATE TITLE: HOW DID I END UP HERE?
SPOILER: DESPERATION.
...AND POSSIBLY MAFIA CONNECTIONS.

Thanks to the solid moral upbringing my parents gave me (you know, the kind that ruled out sex work and pyramid schemes), I ended up in a classroom. Why not? I liked kids. I liked science. I was naive enough to believe I could make a difference.

Many people love to call teaching a "calling." As if it's some sacred vow, whispered to us in a dream by a ghostly nun holding a dry-erase marker.

Let me be clear: I wasn't called. I was cornered. I had just graduated from California State University Long Beach with a shiny Bachelor's in Political Science and a minor in Chemistry, which is basically a degree in over thinking things with a side of lab goggles. I was 22, broke, and allergic to the idea of moving back home.

My parents, ever supportive, took me to dinner with a guy named "Freddy the Leg Breaker." As a kid, when Freddy showed up to talk business with my parents, he'd hand me a quarter and tell me to "go play on the freeway." That was his version of childcare. Now, here I am, a full-grown adult, and still being told to sit quietly while the grown-ups talk, except this time, it was about my future.

Turns out the dinner wasn't about Freddy. It was about his boss, the restaurant owner, a former LAUSD teacher who had seen some shit and gotten out. Freddy leaned in over his calamari and said to me "Call South Fence High School. Ask the secretary if they're looking for a science teacher."

This dinner happened on a Wednesday. On Thursday, I called the school. The principal picked up, asked me to come in that same afternoon, and interviewed me between yelling at students in the hallway.

At this point, I had no teaching credential. No student teaching. No classroom experience. Just a vague understanding of the periodic table and a healthy fear of disappointing my parents.

He hired me on the spot to teach chemistry and told me to start Monday. MONDAY.

That was it. No orientation. No HR packet. Simply a person from admin telling me, "Here's your keys. Room 313. Try not to die."

And just like that, I was in it. Sink or swim, but with teenagers, Bunsen burners, and district mandates written by people who hadn't seen a classroom since Reagan was in office.

That's how I "answered the call." With zero clue, zero preparation, and a stack of outdated textbooks covered in (what I hope was only) gum.

I ended up in a classroom. I liked kids. I liked science. And I was still naive enough to believe I could make a difference.

Spoiler alert: I did.

But what was the price? Astronomical.

I'm talking about missed birthdays, permanent dark circles, and an emotional support water bottle and a constant low-grade hum of burnout.

I made a difference. But I also made ulcer tissue, nervous tics, and a new personality disorder or two.

So when people say teaching is a "calling," I laugh. Because if this were a "calling," it came from a blocked number, and I was too broke not to pick up.

 A Note to Parents:

The new teacher doesn't need you to "check in;" we need you to login to the school portal.

A Note to Administration (Admin):

On their first day, consider giving new employees (at a minimum) a student handbook, whiteboard markers, the teacher version of the textbook, laptop and phone number to IT. Ideally, you could also provide a copy of the curriculum, a bell schedule, and an appointment with IT during prep period to set everything up. A dream would be a printer, with toner and paper, so the teacher could print the assignment and then make copies. (Where do we make copies? NO IDEA. If no printer is available for the classroom, where do we print?)

I Found My Calling to Be a Teacher

I heard the call.
Too bad it was a prank call.

CLASSROOM COMBAT
(MINUS THE ACTUAL COMBAT PAY)

by Dr. Dana

TEACHER

Chapter 2

Twenty Years of Classroom Combat, (Minus the Actual Combat Pay).

That year, when I started teaching, I asked my colleagues why there was a random opening at this time of the year. This school was year-round, and the staff was there for years, so there were rarely any openings. My classroom was on the third floor of an all-brick building overlooking the courtyard. No one wanted to answer that question until months into the position.

I started in September, and by November, someone finally told me the story—the legend, really—of our principal. It was mid-July, and he was on his usual morning stroll through the courtyard. Peaceful. Predictable. Except, on this particular day, desks and chairs were flying out of my classroom window. Yes, flying three floors down, soaring into the courtyard with all the grace of a Broadway finale and the soundtrack of a scrapyard symphony. And what did my calm, collected principal do? He adjusted his tie, gracefully stepped around a crashing chair, and walked straight into my classroom. Without missing a beat, he looked around at the remaining students and asked, "Where's your teacher?"

They pointed silently to the storage closet. Because obviously, that's where teachers go to cry and hide.

I've heard different versions of what he found there. Some say the poor guy was curled up in a corner, others swear he was dangling from the rafters like a Bunsen burner in a windstorm. Either way, the ambulance showed up, gently escorted him out, and wheeled him off to a room with padded walls and a fashionable white jacket with straps.

I don't remember his name. But I do know that if it weren't for that breakdown, I wouldn't have started my teaching career. This was the teacher that let me inherit his classroom, his students and even his original desk from the school opened in the early 1900s.

"Calling"? My ass! I needed a job.

And, again, thanks to the solid moral up bringing my parents gave me (you know, the kind that discouraged sex work, pyramid schemes, and dating DJs), I tried to keep it respectable.

I even bought knee pads once. Not for that; get your mind out of the gutter. They were for metaphorical groveling, but I still couldn't bring myself to take the price tag off. Because deep down, I knew: I wasn't brave enough to be a sellout. Just desperate enough to teach.

Now that I'm 44, I don't really have the body for porn, but I do have an MBA and, turns out, the adult film industry is always looking for someone to manage payroll. So at least there's that backup plan.

So if you're here expecting a happy tale of transformation, one of those "they grow up and will thank you one day" stories, go read *Chicken Soup for the Teacher's Soul*.

This book? This is what's left after the soup boils off and the kitchen catches fire.

This was back in the early 2000s, so being in a brick building meant no cell phone reception; however, the classroom had a traditional phone on the wall that went directly to the office. Now know this: South Fence had 4,000 students, almost 300 staff members, and one person answering the phone. Of course, one person answering the phone is adequate enough for this level of teenage mayhem.

I was 22 straight out of college, I had my life ahead of me! I was naive enough to believe that one day I would get married, have kids, and have a house with a white picket fence, but not today.

I tried going to law school. Long story short: I made an emotional decision and was not able to finish law school, so I needed a job for this gap year, so I could re apply for law school. Imagine my surprise when one day one of my students (I think she was 15; we will call her Julia) walked into my classroom with some news. She was 9 months pregnant! During the nutrition break I calmly walked over to my department chair's room and asked him for help.

"Did I mention Julia was 9 months pregnant?"

My department chair looked at me and asked if I received the daily newspaper in my classroom. I said yes. He then asked, "Do you know how to boil water?" Ah, I get it: I would need to have baby delivering skills when Julia's day and time comes. I walked out of his room.

I told Julia to stay home and to call me every morning. I would mark her present; that way, I wouldn't have to worry about her going into labor in my classroom. I felt like this was in the best interest of everyone involved. Now, I know my "calling" is to deliver babies, to develop cell phone reception, or to teach, depending on who you asked. Who's complaining? I am sure that if I were an engineer or accountant, I might also have to deliver a baby while doing my "normal" daily work.

To this day, my mom keeps telling me not to complain about teaching. I make good money, and I have the summers off. However, she hasn't spent one day in the classroom.

Twenty years later, I make six figures, $104,000. I had to get two master's degrees and a doctorate just to hit that salary. If we are running the numbers and want to see ROI, we need to look at the really big picture. I accumulated over $100,000 in student debt at 6% interest, basically a second mortgage for the privilege of teaching in a room with windows that no longer open, broken air conditioning, and 38 hormonal teenagers who fact-check me mid-sentence with TikToks and Wikipedia; without a working copier within a five-mile radius. Worst of all, the curriculum is written by people who haven't met a teenager since 1987. And, yippee, a yearly raise that barely covers the cost of dry shampoo and ibuprofen. But hey, at least I get to bring my own paper.

But sure. I "make good money."

That "good money?" Yeah. It disappears under a mountain of student loan payments, union dues, classroom supplies (un-reimbursed), and therapy I had to start after the third student death. Yes, you read that correctly. The third student who died while I was teaching, who called me their teacher, who I submitted grades for. But still, I'm expected to be grateful, humble, and fulfilled. (Fulfilled? I haven't peed since 7:15 this morning.)

If you say you "support teachers" and want to really walk the talk: drop off some Clorox wipes at the front office; label it "for a teacher." Or, bring a ream of paper; we'll fight over it like it's Black Friday at Staples. The WWF is nothing compared to teachers who need a ream of paper.

Do you "support teachers?" Really? Do you respect teachers? Let me guess... Your mom was a teacher? Your first boyfriend's twin sister was a teacher? You met a teacher once?

If you really want to support teachers, here's a radical idea: when I call your office during my 15-minute nutrition break to talk to a doctor, or make an appointment, pick up the phone!

I only have 15 minutes.

Yes, your office is busy. Yes, you are important. But I would also like to:

1. Pee.
2. Eat the Snickers bar in my bag

Because if I don't do it now, it won't happen for another four hours.

 ## A Note to Adults:

Teachers cannot pee. Not whenever they want. To pee, I have to leave the classroom. If I leave, no one is watching my students.

So we hold it.

All of it.

Sometimes all day.

#DependsAreTeachersBestFriends

A Note to Admin and District Offices:

When I call in sick, I am sick! No, you cannot have a doctor's note! No, I do not have a sub plan! My mental health is as important as my physical health. How can I help students when I am not healthy enough to take care of myself? On airplanes, we are told to put our mask on before helping others; can we please learn from the airlines? Can you please respect me enough to trust when I call in sick, that I'm really sick?

 ## A Note to Doctors:

When an educator calls your office and says, "I need a sick note for my employer," just give it to us. No, we don't need to be seen. No, we're not contagious. But yes, we need time to avoid collapsing in front of 38 teenagers. Write the note and say we're "under care." (For all anyone knows, it's Pink Eye.)

If you're not going to give me the note, you might as well print "I'd like you to burn all your sick days, then drag yourself back half-dead" on your business card. And remember: When you burn out as a doctor, you can always become a teacher.

SUMMER OFF
What Society Thinks Teachers Do During the Summer

BUT YOU GET SUMMERS OFF!

Here's the thing no one tells you when you start teaching: You're not just expected to do the job, you're expected to look like you're enjoying it at all times.

You can be drowning in paperwork, fighting off a sinus infection, surviving on a granola bar and cold caffeine, while managing three students in an active crisis, and I don't mean they forgot a pencil.

Here's a staunch real-life example from a day of teaching: one is sobbing under a desk because their dad got arrested last night, another is pacing the back of the room, fists clenched, breathing heavy, and the third just threw a chair because someone looked at them "wrong." And still, you better be smiling :)

Because joy is part of the performance. If you look tired, someone's going to suggest "self-care." If you look upset, they'll whisper that you're burned out. If you dare to look human, you might not be "a good fit."

So you smile. You put on the show. You act like teaching during chaos is your passion. Like the chair narrowly missing your whiteboard was just a quirk that happened on a Tuesday.

And then when the bell rings, you reset. Because Period 4 is coming in and they expect a fresh-faced Disney character who loves teaching.

Don't just teach.

Be enthusiastic.

Don't just survive the day.

Be inspirational.

Don't just hold it together after a student tells you to f*** off.

Model emotional regulation with grace and patience.

We don't question when a firefighter retires after 20 years of trauma, or shame ER nurses who walk away from burnout, but when a teacher says, "I can't do this anymore," the response is, "But the kids need you."

The truth is, this system was built to run on martyrdom; it only works if we keep doing it "for the love." Anything less and you're "not a team player" or, worse, you're seen as "negative." God forbid you show frustration, because that's labeled "low morale," and we can't have low morale, can we? That's contagious. Just don't expect me to smile and clap while I drown in debt, burnout, and experience administrative gaslighting, all in the name of a "calling I never actually signed up for."

"But You Get Summers Off!"

Ah, yes, the classic comeback to every teacher's complaint: "But you get summers off."

Do we? Do we really?

Let me take you on a tour of the glamorous, envy-inducing teacher summer: the unpaid weeks where we're scrambling for side gigs because we need to make rent, having to complete professional development we didn't ask for, re-doing lesson plans because the district adopted a new curriculum, and catching up on all the medical appointments we couldn't take during the school year because someone had to watch your kids. It's not a vacation: it's a pit stop in the world's most exhausting relay race, and the baton we're handed in August is already on fire.

Let me break down a teacher's "luxurious summer" for you... minus the luxury.

Week 1: You crash. Hard. You sleep like it's your full-time job. Twelve, sometimes fourteen hours a day.

REALITY:
WHAT TEACHERS ACTUALLY DO
DURING THE SUMMER

Not because you're lazy, no, this is deep-bone exhaustion, the kind studied in medical journals. Your body is trying to recover from nine months of sleep deprivation, caffeine dependency, institutional gaslighting, and children who think "Miss, I finished" means they get to watch YouTube for 40 minutes.

You don't nap; you black out. You wake up at 2:00 PM disoriented, sweating, and unsure of what year it is. Your sheets smell like anxiety and dry shampoo. You dream of unfinished IEPs (Individual Education Plans). Jolting awake, you're convinced you forgot to submit grades. Checking your laptop, you realize that it's summer. You eat cereal for dinner. Not because you're quirky, you eat cereal because dishes feel like too much responsibility, and they also cut into the amount of time you get to sleep. Your eyes twitch involuntarily and your resting heart rate spikes when you hear a bell or the Google Classroom notification sound.

Your body is still in fight-or-flight. But there's nothing to fight. And nowhere left to flee.

Week 2: You clean. Not because you're organized, because this is the only part of your life you can control right now. You attack your house with the ferocity of someone who just watched a Netflix documentary about hoarders. You find cups under your bed, essays in your trunk, and a stack of detention slips in your glove compartment. You wash every hoodie, vacuum under every couch cushion, and finally throw away that stack of unclaimed student work that's been haunting your backseat like ghost mail.

You start your "summer off" by cleaning out your inbox. You're down to 74 unread emails, which feels Zen compared to the 1,367 you had back in April. You finally reply to someone's text from April with "OMG, I just saw this!" like you weren't actively ignoring everyone who didn't work on your campus. No wonder no one dated me this year; I should probably return texts.

You call your dentist, finally book that pap smear and show up to appointments wearing real pants. The front desk receptionist looks genuinely surprised and says, "We thought you died." In my head, I'm thinking, I wish I did, but instead I smile politely and say, "No, I was busy teaching."

You look around and think, Okay. I might be a human again.

Until you realize: Pre-planning starts in four weeks. And you already have two Professional Developments (PDs) scheduled.

Weeks 3 to 6: Professional development. Curriculum writing. Mandatory summer school. And, of course, district training, where some consultant with zero classroom experience tells you how to "engage students through rigor and relationships" while reading directly from a PowerPoint passed down from one tired administrator to another since 2003.

You're sitting in a beige, un-air-conditioned room on a metal folding chair that was clearly designed for a smaller species, surrounded by equally dead-eyed teachers who are all pretending to take notes but are actually playing Wordle or updating their resumes. The only thing keeping you upright is the sad Costco muffin on your lap, as if carbohydrates could somehow make the three-hour presentation more tolerable.

The consultant drones on about "best practices," quoting research they definitely pulled from a TED Talk, while your brain quietly whispers, "Is this what rock bottom feels like?" They drop the word "whole-child," and you feel your soul leave your body.

But you nod. You smile. Because someone will be walking around with an observation sheet that relates to the "whole-child" with phrases such as "engaged," "collaborative," and "growth mindset."

No one asks what your mindset is. No one asks how it feels to sit through your seventh training where the solution is always more data—never more resources, never more staff, never more sanity.

Just rigor. And relationships. And muffins. At least they are Costco muffins.

Week 7: You cry in a Target aisle because back-to-school displays are already up and you still have $40,000 left on your student loans.

REALITY:
What Teachers Actually Do During the Summer

Week 8: You spend every remaining hour, and dollar, prepping your classroom. You hot-glue things to bulletin boards. You organize supply bins like you're auditioning for The Home Edit. You buy folders, snacks, tissues, decorations, and hand sanitizer in bulk because if you don't, no one will. You label everything, color-code, and make it cute. You pretend it's fun. And here's the real kicker: there's no paid time for any work we do before the kids walk into our classroom.

You're expected to make magic happen on your own time, before school starts, after PD, or during the sacred buy-back days, where maybe, if you're lucky, they give you an entire 45 minutes at the end of a five-hour training to prep your classroom.

More often, they suggest that you "use your lunch," because nothing screams productivity like trying to rearrange desks and hang a word wall while inhaling a granola bar and dodging a safety stapler that falls when you are standing on a desk trying to staple and hold the paper while you eat your granola bar at the same time.

So you stay late and come in early. You drag your own children into the building just to spend hours setting up a space that is warm, welcoming, and full of personality, because you've been told that your classroom environment reflects your level of care.

We make door decorations out of butcher paper like it's a sacred craft and act like it's fulfilling instead of humiliating. It's never empowering to be judged on font choices and border trim.

You spend a paycheck at Target, another one at Dollar Tree, and somehow still end up needing more bins. And through all of this, not one hour of it is paid because, apparently, love for the job is supposed to be enough compensation.

But sure, Mom. Tell me again how lucky I am that I get the summer off.

**DON'T WORRY THE DISTRICT SAYS,
BULLET HOLES COUNT AS VENTILATION**

by Dr Dana

Chapter 4

TAKE A BUBBLE BATH AND SHUT UP: SELF-CARE SATURDAY AND OTHER CORPORATE LIES

Let's talk about the latest trend in public education: "wellness." Because when schools are crumbling, classes are overflowing, paychecks barely scrape by, and your HVAC is held together with hope and duct tape, the solution isn't better conditions. It's yoga and a mindfulness app. It's a laminated flyer that says "You Can't Pour from an Empty Cup," handed to you right before they dump a gallon of everyone else's trauma into your personal space.

We've got Wellness Wednesdays, Self-Care Saturdays, and "trauma-informed" initiatives that all sound lovely, until you realize what they actually mean.

Self-Care Saturday: You wake up early, on your day off, to drive to a school site you've never seen before. You walk into a sweltering multipurpose room with no AC and get handed that Costco muffin. Water? No need; there's a rust-flavored fountain from 1986 in the hallway. You're asked to journal, breathe, stretch, and "regulate your nervous system," all while silently screaming about the pile of grading waiting for you and the fact that, come Monday, you'll be regulating everyone else's nervous system too.

They call it "wellness." We call it unpaid labor. There are laws that apply to working without wages, they just don't apply to teachers.

Then there is the "trauma-informed" training, which boils down to the same message we receive with every other training: You are now expected to be a teacher, therapist, crisis counselor, emotional sponge, and trauma expert. Still without a raise. Still without AC. Still without bottled water. Because apparently, your love for kids is supposed to hydrate you too.

There's always a workshop.

Such as this one: "Finding Joy in the Crisis".

Spoiler: The 'chaos' is the job.

And the 'joy'? Left the chat in 2019.

And, of course: Staff Appreciation Week. Donuts on Monday. A "You Rock!" sticky note on Tuesday. A 175-page testing protocol packet on Wednesday.

We don't need chair yoga. We need chairs that aren't broken.

We don't need breathing exercises. We need 45 minutes of silence to eat a meal that didn't come out of our desk drawer or get swallowed between a fight in 3rd period and a parent email that starts with "As a taxpayer…"

And stop telling us to "set boundaries." As if this job has an off switch. (Sure, let me try this line out: "Hey kiddo, I know you're having a panic attack, but my therapist says I need to protect my peace. Circle back during contract hours, okay?")

You can't "boundary" your way out of systemic failure. You can't meditate your way out of poverty, disrespect, and a job that requires you to be a social worker, cop, tech support, nurse, data analyst, party planner, and punching bag, all before lunch.

But hey, light a candle. Take a walk and color a mandala. By the way, make sure to shut the hell up about your burnout. Because when you collapse at your desk from a heart attack, they'll have a sub in your seat before the body is cold, and definitely before the copier cools down.

by Dr Dana

Hydrate.

I wish that were just a punchline. But it's not.

In my third year of teaching, I worked at a school on the west side of L.A. Every morning, I got there early to race the math teacher to the copier. We bonded over paper jams and caffeine, which were just enough sarcasm to survive the day. One morning, he beat me there. We joked, wished each other a good day. He went to his classroom. I stayed to make my copies.

From my window, I saw the ambulance arrive. I didn't even flinch because at schools, ambulances are like pigeons in parking lots: always around, mildly concerning, but mostly ignored.

Later, I found out that the math teacher I was just joking with at the copier had a heart attack at his desk. He fell over when his heart failed and hit his head. After he collapsed, two kids walked in for tutoring and found him on the floor. That's how their day started: pre-algebra and post-trauma.

He never woke up.

But don't worry, the district moved quickly. A sub was in his room within 15 minutes. And by the end of the week? A shiny new teacher, smiling and passing out syllabi like nothing ever happened.

What about the kids' grief and their trauma? How about acknowledging the loss to their fellow teachers? None of this was on the agenda. No funeral, grief processing, or time to pay honors to a teacher who dedicated his life to children The only kudos he received was a minute of silence squeezed in before an announcement about testing windows.

He died at school. And the machine kept running.

So seriously: take care of yourself. Because they will replace you faster than a toner cartridge.

And if you're a civilian (a massage therapist, a spa scheduler, a nail tech) reading this, listen up: When a teacher calls you for an appointment, move mountains to make it happen. Don't book the 4:00 slot unless you are a teacher. If you're sitting in that chair and you're not one of us, you didn't just take a massage, you took our one shot at feeling human again. So don't say you "support teachers." You just stole our damn appointment. And honestly?

You suck!

So if you say you support teachers, do so in actions, not just words.

by Dr Dana

NOT CONFUSED. JUST LAZY. THAT'S NOT A LEARNING ISSUE. THAT'S A PARENTING ISSUE.

MY CHILD WOULD NEVER...
BUT HE JUST DID.

Look, I get it. You love your child. You made him. You feed him. You tuck him in. He's got your smile. He's your whole heart.

But let me say this clearly, with all the love and truth in the world: Your child is not that special.

He is lying to you. He is not doing his work. And the reason you're getting those emails? It's not because I'm out to get him. It's because he's blowing off assignments and then telling you that I'm the problem. Or worse, he's got your email sign-in and is deleting the emails I'm sending you and then emptying your trash in your email so you won't find them, even if you search for my email address.

These aren't made-up stories; these are real-life, in-the-trenches teacher experiences that we have regularly.

You don't need to schedule a conference or send me an email asking for "clarification" when your child isn't doing well in my class. You don't even need to leave a voicemail where you pretend to be confused.

Open his backpack. Login to Schoology. Ask him questions about his class, what his responsibilities are and, for God's sake, look at the syllabus I gave him at the beginning of the school year! You know: the one you signed, but didn't read?

If he doesn't want you in his backpack, or on his account, or seeing what's in his Chrome history, it's not because he is "respecting anyone's privacy." It's because he's hiding something. Parenting your child doesn't equate to giving him carte blanche to do whatever he pleases on the Internet. That's what predators who stalk children want. And I'm sure you don't want your child in that situation, do you?

And, let me say this, too: If your kid is hiding porn or drugs in his backpack, and I, the teacher, am the one who finds it...

- I'm not lying. Let's be clear: I have better porn and drug access than your 16-year-old and zero incentive to make this up.

- Why am I the one finding it? Seriously. What kind of shitty parenting are you doing if your child is walking into my classroom with a blunt and a USB drive full of porn, and you're still emailing me about their "participation grade?" Oh, I see, you're not talking about his participation inside of looking at pornography?

- If you're offended by this, it's probably true. So go check their bag. Their room, and especially their texts. They are under 18, so they don't have the privilege of privacy. You're responsible for every illegal act they take part in. You're the parent. ACT LIKE ONE.

The problem is either the child or the parent! Most times, I would put money on the parents.

If you've ever wanted to know what it feels like to be both a customer service rep and the product, welcome to the magical world of parent-teacher communication. It's where logic goes to die and expectations go to hell.

Every child is somehow God's gift to mankind, a misunderstood prodigy who's been tragically wronged by cruel insistence on expectations and responsibilities such as due dates, instructions, and reality.

"My child would never lie." Ma'am, your child is lying right now while eating hot Cheetos in class and streaming TikTok on 12 tabs on their smartphone.

Parent: "I know he didn't turn in any work, but can he still pass?"

Teacher: "Sure. And I'll just invoice the Tooth Fairy for the missing assignments."

Parent: Can you just let him retake the test, and also, he's at Disneyland?"

Teacher: No problem. I'll deliver it personally between the Matterhorn ride and Space Mountain.

But the real kicker? The tone. That thin, patronizing smile. That "I'm just confused why" tone that usually comes before a veiled threat about going to the school board. Oh, and then the best part: the performance review you didn't ask for.

"It just seems like you don't understand my child." Lady. Your child is sixteen. You have one; I've had at least 120 sixteen-year-olds every single year for the past 14 years. That's over 1,600 teenagers, but sure, you, with your one angry sophomore who thinks The Great Gatsby is a shoe brand, clearly understand this age group better than I do.

"But he's special." You're right. He's special. So, so special. So special that, somehow, none of the basic expectations of high school should apply to him, such as deadlines, acceptable behavior, or showing up with pants. And, don't worry; I've never seen anyone like him. He's truly unique in how he hasn't turned in a single assignment and still thinks he should be getting a B "for effort."

"Why didn't you tell me he was failing?" I did. I emailed, called and posted grades on that platform that you have access to, but never log in to for some reason. I printed a progress report and mailed a letter home with a sticker and a prayer. But now that we're here, four days before finals, it's suddenly my fault your son forgot there was homework in this class. Or any class for that matter.

"You don't believe in him." No, I believe he can pass. I also believe he needs to do his classwork and pass his tests to make that happen. You know, show up to class, do the homework, stop cussing me out. (I would settle for two out of the three. Call me radical.)

And then we have the pièce de résistance: the Parent-Teacher Conference, that sacred theater performance where we all sit around a tiny table and pretend little Jason is just misunderstood and not a menace with a vape pen and a body count in Kahoot (on online game to learning, like Bingo but digitalized). You tell me he's never like this at home, that he's a good kid, and the behavior I'm describing doesn't sound like him. Meanwhile, he's across from me, chewing gum like it owes him money and asking if this will "go on his permanent record." But, yes, I'm sure the problem is me.

Teachers aren't just fighting for learning outcomes; we're doing triage on kids who show up every day with trauma, lies, and in some cases, loaded weapons in their backpacks.

Let me tell you about the time a loaded gun (yes, a gun with the safety off) was in a backpack and went off in the classroom. A 14-year-old brought a weapon to school and I, the science teacher, had to deal with it. So, while you're worried about whether I'm "being nice" to your child, know that I'm struggling to stay alive in my classroom, which is the main focus of my day. I'm actively trying not to die!

You know what would show me you respect me as an educator?

Parent your precious child.

They don't need a cheerleader. They need:

- Rules.
- Oversight.
- Consequences.
- And, they need to know they can't manipulate you into emailing me to cover for them.

 A Note to Parents:

Open your student's backpack, have your student log in to Schoology, AeriesAERIES, or whatever grading platform your school uses. If your student tells you the school/teacher/society does not use a Learning Management System (LMS), then contact the administration to verify that they are correct. Don't assume your child is telling you the truth. They want to cover up their lack of responsibility and place it on the teacher. You have to be adept enough to figure out that your child is trying to pull a fast one on you and make you look bad. Take your student's computer and look at the tabs they have used. Check their history! The teacher and parent work best if they are allies. The teacher knows more about your kid's daily interactions than any parent because we are here, seeing their every move.

**SURE I'LL TRACK YOUR STUDENT
BETWEEN RIDES.**

Professional development:
because waterboarding is illegal.

PROFESSIONAL DEVELOPMENT – WHERE LOGIC GOES TO DIE.

Let's be clear: Professional Development isn't some once-a-semester all-day event where you fake enthusiasm through a six-hour slideshow on trauma-informed icebreakers.

In my world, PD happens every damn Tuesday after school for one hour of mandatory, unpaid time. Nothing says "we respect teachers" like forcing them to stay late without pay to learn something they could have Googled in four minutes or a topic they already know about because they've been doing the job for 14 years.

By the time Tuesday rolls around, I've already been teaching on fumes for two days. I've broken up a fight, refilled my own printer ink, counseled a sobbing teenager, called a parent who didn't answer, and chased a bird out of the hallway. I am done.

But instead of going home, grading, or just sitting in silence like a war veteran processing the day, I'm in the library with 137 other exhausted teachers pretending to care about "building a more culturally responsive classroom community through exit tickets."

We're not getting paid. But we are getting a handout. Sometimes cookies. Once, a highlighter. One time someone brought La Croix and acted like it was a salary.

You want to know what kind of growth I'm doing in these meetings? I'm growing resentful. I'm growing a stress ulcer. I'm growing a secret fantasy of getting up, walking out, and never coming back.

But I stay, because it's "collaborative," and because the union contract says I technically can't leave until 3:45 PM. Because if I don't show up, I'm "not a team player." And if I show up but stop participating, I'm "not solution-oriented."

It's a trap.

And don't get me started on the "strategies" they introduce as if they're groundbreaking: Let's try sentence frames! Been using those since 2009. How about grouping by data? That's called differentiated instruction, you are welcome. Have you heard of Think-Pair-Share? Yes. It's literally on the wall of every sixth-grade classroom in America.

The worst part? They act like they're doing us a favor. Like we should be grateful they're "investing in our development." You want to invest in me? Let me go home. Let me take a nap, drink some water, and not talk about vertical alignment with three people who have been grading the entire meeting anyway. Or, better yet: pay me.

"But you're done at 3:00 PM!"

Totally. I'm so done at 3:00 PM. Yeah, I'm out the door at 3:00 PM on the dot, sipping iced tea on a porch swing and reading romance novels, just like everyone imagines.

Did I mention the time a gun went off in a backpack? Now, I spend my weekends at the gun range, learning how to take out the magazine, clear the barrel, and put on the safety. Because let's be real: the crisis in schools isn't "instructional development" or "vertical alignment." It's not about standards or pacing guides. It's about life-or-death safety.

Do you know how many teachers can operate a firearm? How many can identify the signs of a fentanyl overdose? How many even know what fentanyl looks like?

We don't talk about that in PD. But, sure, let's keep reviewing the difference between "Depth of Knowledge Level 2" and "Level 3", while a student in the back row of my 3rd period just Googled how to make a homemade vape.

A Note to Districts and Admin:

If you want "useful professional development," maybe start offering a session on how to neutralize a gun. Or, if that feels too extreme, at least give us the option of PD on actual social-emotional development. Dealer's choice.

Let's just play it out, hypothetically.

Imagine every teacher is trained. We all know how to clar a gun. We know how to apply the safety and we're not afraid of firearms.

Now picture this: A student, a community member, parent, or another individual walks into my classroom with a weapon. (That would never happen, right? Just like the other schools that had mass shootings, because we all know that school security is infallible.) Hypothetically, I calmly approach, smile, offer to gently take the weapon, apply the safety, set it down, and no one is injured.

Or, here's the more likely version:

A gunman walks into my classroom. I freeze. Because I'm a science teacher, not a SWAT officer. I start screaming. The kids start screaming. The gunman starts shooting. There are injuries — and most likely deaths.

But hey, at least I completed my district-mandated Social Emotional Learning module. At least I passed the quiz on mindfulness. At least I know that when a student is melting down, I'm supposed to say, "I can see that you're having big feelings right now." Because that will definitely stop a bullet.

PROFESSIONAL DEVELOPMENT
BINGO *by* Dr. Dana

300-slide PowerPoint

Icebreaker

Icebreaker

Mandatory Evaluation Form

Collect no evaluation

BINGO!

PBIS	MTSS	PLC	DIFFER-ENTIATION	EQUITY
BEST PRACTICES	STUDENT ENGAGEMENT	TRAUMA INFORMED	LIFELONG LEARNERS	NEW INITIATIVE
SOCIAL EMOTIONAL LEARNING	SATURDAY TRAINING	FREE SPACE	PD	SSC
IEP	STUDENT NEEDS	PARKING LOT	BUZZWORD OF THE DAY	MORE WORK SAME PAY
DATA-DRIVEN	'PARKI-NG LOT	BUZZWORD OF THE DAY	"WE VALUE TEACHERS"	MANDATORY FUN

by Dr Dana

FIRST ONE TO BURNOUT WINS!

 A Note to Teachers:

Feel free to play this BINGO card at your next PD. First one to BURNOUT wins! Or not?

by Dr Dana

HIRE ME. I'VE ALREADY
BEEN TO HELL, IN FLATS.

Fourteen years. That's over 2,500 school days. Roughly 25,000 class periods filled with thousands of student interactions, fire drills, lockdowns, missing bathroom passes, and passive-aggressive emails from parents who think "he's trying" is an acceptable substitute for "It's May, and he hasn't turned in anything since Halloween."

And somehow, I didn't bite anyone. (Anyone that I'm willing to admit on the record.)

You know that phrase, "If you can make it here, you can make it anywhere?" They were talking about public school teachers. Because, if you can survive a June classroom with 37 overheated sophomores, two broken ceiling fans, one kid who just discovered Axe body spray, and another spiraling into a narcissistic meltdown, you can survive anything.

We've taught through pandemics, grief, broken tech, broken systems and broken spirits. We were told to be calm under pressure, warm but not too soft, firm but not too mean, consistent yet flexible, fun but not unprofessional, inspirational but test-aligned and emotionally available at all times. Oh, and don't forget to take attendance.

We smiled through heartbreak. We've taught standards that were given to us without our input, using tools that didn't work, under evaluations we couldn't control, to students we weren't allowed to discipline. And, then, someone in administration or the district had the audacity to ask why morale was low.

But we still showed up. Taught during our prep, coached during our lunch, cried in our cars, wiped our faces, and walked back in with a smile. We bought snacks and remembered birthdays. We wrote letters of recommendation and stayed late to help kids rewrite essays, re-do labs, and restart their lives.

And somehow, we held on to our sanity, our standards, and our last working whiteboard marker.

We may be tired; we may flinch when we hear "walkthrough," "benchmark," or "new initiative." But we made it, and that counts for something. Because the corporate world loves to brag about resilience, grit, leadership, and conflict resolution. The corporate world thinks they've got the upper hand on these soft skills but, baby, we wrote the book on them!

We led troops into academic warfare armed only with whiteboards and granola bars. We resolved conflicts that would make HR departments spontaneously combust. We stayed calm while children cursed, sobbed, and, yes, once built a fort out of lab goggles and an iPad.

So the next time someone says, "Oh, you were just a teacher?" I just smile and say: "No. I was a crisis-tested, multi-hat-wearing, cross-functional operations specialist with expertise in education, compliance, behavior intervention, and live performance under hostile conditions for 14 years. I was the first responder, project manager, crisis negotiator, event coordinator, compliance officer, and stand-up comic who happened to work in a building with a bell schedule. And I did it without hazard pay, body armor, or a marketing department."

STILL SMILING...

Burnout Isn't a Buzzword, It's a Diagnosis

No, a bubble bath won't fix the teaching issues.

They love to throw around the word "burnout" like it's a quirky phase. Like it's something you shake off with a weekend nap and some self-care on Saturday. But what they don't tell you is this: burnout isn't just "tired," it's a full system shutdown.

by Dr Dana

It's when you forget your passwords. When you cry in a Costco parking lot because you forgot eggs and can't afford to go back. It's staring at a stack of ungraded papers and realizing you physically can't care anymore, even though you want to.

Burnout is when your body starts making decisions without you. You forget words, lose names and feel nothing. A student tells you their grandma died, and you just nod because you don't have the energy to react.

And the worst part? You don't even realize how bad it's gotten until you're done. Until you sleep for three days and your hair stops falling out. You know you're getting past burnout when you can look at a calendar and not feel the urge to scream.

Because in education, burnout is normalized. It's disguised as "dedication." It's praised in staff meetings. It's baked into the calendar, with three-day weekends offered like humanitarian aid after you've worked 12-hour days for two months straight.

You're told to practice "self-care," while being asked to:
- Stay late for tutoring,
- Grade during your prep,
- Show up for the kids,
- Track 8,000 data points, and
- Not complain.

But one should also be joyful, inspiring, and deeply invested at all times. So, yeah, I burned out. Not because I was weak, but because I was strong for way too long. And, in the peak of that burnout spiral, I said 'yes' to a new assignment: a community day school.

If you don't know what that is, let me explain: It's where students go when expulsion is on the table or when life has hit so hard, traditional schools no longer serve them.

I thought I could do this. I've got science credentials. (Not one, but two!) I am a fully-credentialed biology teacher and chemistry teacher. I've got experience and grit.

I also have a 200-pound frame on a 5-foot body, a doctor who's concerned about my cholesterol, and a Google search history full of diets that I started but never finished, because I'm a teacher.

So when a staff member, my principal to be specific, looked at me and said with a straight face, "You look like an athlete. You should coach PE," I blinked, laughed and replied: "Great! As a pack-a-day smoker, I'm sure I'll be an incredible role model."

Apparently, sarcasm wasn't a second language on that campus.

Next thing I knew, I was assigned to teach Health. Because clearly, what I needed during a nervous breakdown was one more prep I wasn't credentialed for. Sorry, not just one prep, two preps, because they wanted me to teach middle school health and high school health.

But this is what burnout looks like in real time. You say 'yes' to the absurd, because you've been brainwashed to make it work. You take on roles you're not qualified for, because someone has to, right?

But somehow I held court in that room. I taught and laughed. I made those students believe someone still gave a damn. It wasn't perfect, but it was real.

And I realized something: Leadership isn't about looking the part, it's about showing up. Even when the copier's jammed, even when the data makes no sense, even when your doctor says you're one bad meal away from becoming a solid and even when your principal confuses you for a Division-I athlete.

So no, I didn't just make it to year fourteen. I dragged myself there, with sarcasm, science, and exactly zero confirmed bite marks.

But, don't worry: I get the summers off.

  A Note to Admin:

Last year I was at a community day school which was an interesting use of public funds. This school paid for salaries for four teachers, six counselors, three classified helpers, one office manager, one custodian, one Assistant Principal, and one Principal for 56 students. At a traditional high school there might be 100 teachers, but you still have six counselors, three classified helpers, one office manager, one custodian, one Assistant Principal, and one Principal.

The community day school included students grades 7th–12th. In the same classroom at the same time. Maybe we should look at a different option, instead of the current one that places a misbehaved 7th grader in a room with a 12th grader (18-year-old) who only has 9th grade credits. Spoiler: the 12th grader either gets annoyed by the 7th grader or just found a new lackey to do his bidding on the street. (Is that what society meant when they said "no child left behind?")

Imagine having a detention room on every campus. Since the community day school has so many classes at the same time in the same room, the dean, who is already on campus, could supervise the student working independently on assignments. The counselors who are already on campus can pull the kid easier and help them. They are not affecting other students, and you don't require an additional four teachers, six counselors, three classified helpers, one office manager, one custodian, one Assistant Principal, and one Principal. I know this would prioritize the students, and adults would have to find jobs at other locations, but aren't we supposed to be helping students?

Chapter 9

Thanks for the Trauma, and the Ulcer. I'll Be Crying in Urgent Care If You Need Me.

I left teaching. I didn't make a scene when I left. No dramatic goodbye, no slideshow, no tearful potluck. I just vanished. Slipped out the back door of a career that devoured me, and all I got was a text asking if I could cover summer school.

After 14 years, I wasn't a person anymore. I was a credential with a pulse. A warm body they could toss into any flaming disaster labeled "coverage needed." I was useful, not valued, dependable, not supported, expected to be everything, everywhere, all at once, on a Chromebook with a cracked screen.

No one noticed I was unraveling when I was juggling lunch duty, a sub shortage, a bathroom monitor shift, and a fire drill, all while trying to teach through the chaos of second period's daily Lord of the Flies reenactment. I'd lost my voice, my patience, and my ability to feel anything beyond caffeine and survival instinct.

Supplies? Forget it. The budget had already been raided, as the History teacher got approval to take students to the marine mammal center to "enhance cross-curricular engagement." When I taught Marine Biology, I was told a whale watching trip wasn't "instructionally defensible" or "standards-aligned." So, instead of seeing actual whales, we stuck to rigorous, evidence-based worksheets. Inspiring. Truly preparing future-ready learners. But, sure, I'm the expensive one. I'm difficult, opinionated, and too much because I dared to ask for desks that didn't wobble like toddlers on sugar.

If I had any energy left, I might've stood on a desk and said: "I'm not leaving because I couldn't handle it. I'm leaving because I handled all of it, and it damn near killed me."

They took away my twenties. My nervous system. My Sundays. My ability to hear the word "rubric" without flinching. They got all of me, the best of me and, in return, I got burnout, betrayal, and a drawer full of dry Expo markers.

I even learned how to disarm a firearm — not because it was in my training but because, at some point, it just became part of the job. Just another Tuesday, another item on the to-do list: "Teach state standards. Provide trauma-informed care. Neutralize threats."

So yeah. I'm done. Done grading in my car. Done crying in Target parking lots. Done being told to "practice mindfulness" while covering three classes. Done being evaluated by someone whose last classroom experience was during a field trip in 2004.

I'm not bitter: I'm awake and clear-eyed. I'm over sacrificing myself. I'm walking away with chronic exhaustion, a nervous twitch, and a wildly inappropriate sense of humor. But I am walking away.

You don't get to label teaching a calling when it leaves you bleeding.

Dear New Teacher,

Aww, look at you: Fresh lanyard, inspirational mug, eyes full of hope.

You think you're going to change lives. That's adorable.

Here's the reality: You're walking into a building on fire, and they'll hand you a squirt gun and a smile. They'll call it a "calling" right before they ask you to cover lunch duty, a fight in the quad, and someone else's class, during your prep.

They'll say "It's all for the kids" while blaming you for the system they refuse to fix. And when you burn out? They'll give you a candle and a flyer that says "Self-Care Starts With You."

So run. Run now. Run fast.

And if you stay? Don't lose your soul trying to prove you have one.

Love,

Someone Who Escaped (with coffee stains and rage).

Apparently managing 200 teenagers isn't management experience.

WHAT TO DO AFTER TEACHING

So I left the classroom. Congratulations! I am now a civilian. I can pee whenever I want, eat warm food and, if I'm lucky, go a full workday without being told someone's ferret died and that's why they're throwing scissors in a high school classroom. I made it.

But now comes the next horror story: the job hunt. Because the second I tried to pivot into a new career, the world suddenly got amnesia. "Oh, you were a teacher?" Yeah. For 14 years. "So, do you have any real experience?"

Oh, you mean besides:
- Managing 160 humans with unpredictable behavior and no legal recourse,
- Writing 100+ lesson plans weekly, aligned to standards, scaffolded, differentiated, and embedded with literacy strategies for multiple levels of fluency and cognitive function,
- Presenting daily to hostile audiences,
- Creating, collecting, and analyzing performance data to identify growth targets and adjust instruction mid-flight,
- Collaborating across departments while also serving as therapist, emergency contact, tech support, conflict mediator, and behavior specialist?

Nope. Nothing real. I don't have any real experience.

Wait, let me translate that for you in Project Management Language:
- Developed and executed 100–120 customized strategic plans per week, aligned to regulatory frameworks and tailored for 5+ tiers of cognitive and language proficiency, resulting in a 20–30% increase in engagement and performance over baseline.

- Facilitated 25+ live presentations per week to resistant and often-disengaged audiences, consistently meeting communication objectives under time constraints and emotionally charged environments.
- Designed and maintained a performance-tracking system, analyzing 10,000+ individual data points annually to identify growth targets, optimize workflows, and drive mid-cycle adjustments that improved outcomes by up to 40% in targeted areas.
- Led cross-functional collaboration with 10+ internal departments, while concurrently providing front-line support in IT troubleshooting, crisis response, emotional triage, compliance navigation, and conflict mediation, reducing escalation incidents by 35%.

They'll ask, "Ever worked in an office?" Well, I've turned in paperwork to five departments on three platforms, mastered Google Suite, ran a class website, filled out behavior logs, wrote incident reports, built budget spreadsheets, tracked parent contacts, and submitted legally binding IEP documentation with 72 acronyms I had to pretend to understand. But sure, let's act like I don't know how email works.

Wait, let me translate that for you, too:
- Managed cross-departmental documentation workflows across 5 departments and 3 digital platforms, ensuring 100% compliance with procedural deadlines and legal standards.
- Utilized advanced proficiency in Google Workspace to streamline communication, resource sharing, and data tracking across multiple stakeholder groups.
- Designed, launched, and maintained an external-facing project website, improving end-user access to resources and reducing inbound inquiries by 40%.
- Generated and submitted 100+ behavior and incident reports, ensuring consistent documentation for risk mitigation and internal review.
- Created and maintained dynamic budget tracking spreadsheets, monitoring resource allocations, and supporting compliance with internal controls.
- Tracked and documented over 500 stakeholder communications annually, using CRM-style systems to ensure accountability and follow-through.
- Completed time-sensitive, legally binding reports containing 70+ regulatory codes and compliance acronyms, meeting all audit and procedural standards under high-pressure timelines.

They'll ask, "What project management experience do you have?" Ever planned an entire semester for 160 teenagers, balancing content, behavior, pacing, testing windows, field trips, accommodations, IEPs, 504s, and whatever fire drill the district threw in at the last minute? That's project management in nightmare mode.

Or, in corporate-speak:

- Planned, scheduled, and executed multi-phase projects spanning 18+ weeks for over 160 end-users, balancing regulatory requirements, content delivery, engagement strategy, and individual accommodations.
- Coordinated simultaneous workflows across 10+ constraint areas, including compliance (IEPs/504s), stakeholder engagement, behavioral risk mitigation, standardized testing logistics, off-site events, and emergency response interruptions.
- Adapted strategic plans in real time to accommodate shifting organizational directives (e.g., last-minute scheduling changes, compliance updates, and system outages), maintaining 95% milestone completion under changing conditions.
- Oversaw full-cycle program management for 160+ participants, including needs assessments, resource allocation, timeline development, outcome tracking, and performance evaluation, resulting in consistent delivery within scope and deadlines.
- Balanced cross-functional priorities across legal, operational, and human-centered domains, with zero violations, escalations, or missed deliverables over multiple project cycles.

But here's the truth they don't want to hear: Teachers are terrifyingly skilled because, to survive our job, we had to be. We're resourceful, emotionally intelligent, fast, adaptable, and freakishly organized under pressure. We can present, lead, track, coach, analyze, synthesize, document, and strategize, all with three hours of sleep and a bloody nose in the back row. So, no, I haven't worked in a corporation or corporate office. But I have had a parent threaten to sue me and still showed up the next day with a color-coded agenda and snacks for the kids who hadn't eaten. The issue isn't our experience. It's that the world has no clue what teaching actually entails and how it tears down people who are teaching.

A Note to Soon-To-Be Former Teachers:

So what do you do after teaching? You translate. You re-brand. You say "stakeholder communication" instead of "calling 19 parents during lunch." You say "project coordination" instead of "building labs with no budget and 38 kids per class." You say "data-driven outcomes" instead of "testing kids who haven't eaten while pretending scores reflect learning." You take every insane overworked thing you ever did, and you give it the language they respect.

Then you walk in and show them what a real professional looks like. Because you weren't "just a teacher." You were an entire organization, running solo, on fumes, with a smile. And if they don't get it? That's their loss.

Certified in trauma and toner replacement.

REJECTED JOB DESCRIPTIONS I'VE ACTUALLY SEEN

Alternate Title: "Apparently I'm Not Qualified to Fold T-Shirts."
After I left the classroom, I dove headfirst into the job hunt with a resume full of leadership, data analysis, conflict resolution, logistics management, trauma counseling, tech skills, and the stamina of a caffeinated raccoon.
And somehow...

They said they wanted someone with a high school diploma. Maybe an associate's degree. I have three master's degrees, a bachelor's, and a doctorate. No associate's degree. Somehow, not having a two-year degree is the issue.

I've spent two decades managing classrooms, budgets, children, adults who act like children, lesson plans, IEPs, and enough chaos to qualify as a first responder in some states. But, apparently, none of that counts. Every time I applied for a job outside of education, I ran into the same wall: "We're looking for someone with at least three years of experience in accounts payable using a proprietary internal invoice matching system." Right. Three years of scanning invoices into a system that no one outside your company has access to for a job that pays $18.27 an hour and requires "strong attention to detail and the ability to lift 30 pounds." Cool.

My experience juggling 150 students, navigating educational law, submitting government reports, managing state funds, and surviving six different superintendents doesn't matter. My degrees are irrelevant. My ability to make miracles happen before noon using a Chromebook, a Band-Aid, and one working projector bulb does not constitute "entry-level."
Meanwhile, here are the jobs I considered, laughed at, and absolutely should've been hired for immediately:

School District Assistant Analyst — $50,000/year – 224 Days – Must Have 3+ Years of Accounts Payable Experience.

Let's break this down, shall we?

- Fifty thousand a year. For 224 workdays, 38 more days than I worked as a teacher. That's nearly six more weeks of labor. For literally half the salary I made teaching ($104,000, thank you very much), and here's the cherry on the gaslit sundae:

- "High school diploma required. Three years of accounts payable experience preferred."

- I have a Doctorate, an MBA, three Master's degrees, and 14 years of experience managing budgets, requisitions, grants, purchasing, and tracking every damn penny in my classroom because if I didn't, no one would. But that doesn't count.

Doesn't count, because I haven't sat in a cubicle for three years entering invoices for someone else's Costco receipts.

Doesn't count, because budgeting lab supplies for 180 students with a $63 annual science allocation (that is a total number, by the way, not a per-child), while maintaining compliance with district and state regulations doesn't teach you anything about financial responsibility.

Got it.

Also, I love how this job is literally in a school district office, and somehow, actual classroom experience is irrelevant. Seriously, this was a job I applied for in a large district, in which they said my experience as a teacher is not equivalent to an account payable position. As if understanding how schools function from the inside is a liability, not a strength.

I am expected to promote college; all graduating students should be college-ready. Why? I went to college, I even graduated (not once, not twice), and have five degrees. I even have a Masters in Business Administration but, you're right, I don't have three years of accounts payable experience. I'm sure I will figure out what is needed before you finish onboarding and I will never ask for help unless it's urgent because I'm literate and I know how to read a book to answer my questions. (Hell, I'm so old, I even know how to use a dictionary.)

Fire Alarm Monitor — "Supervise and assess building safety systems to ensure emergency preparedness." The fire alarm went off almost every day. Sometimes every period. And because I taught chemistry, in a room with open gas lines, I always evacuated. Because, you know... fire.

Every time I followed protocol, I got a passive-aggressive email from my principal about "wasting instructional time." Meanwhile, I was following federal safety code CFR Title 29 §1910.38, which requires immediate evacuation during an unverified alarm in a hazardous environment. That's right, it's the law.

Because if I stayed and there was a fire? I'd be responsible for frying thirty-six children and a tray of half-finished copper sulfate experiments. If it's not a fire? Great. I get to circle up on the blacktop like it's recess in

by Dr Dana

Evacuate in a calm, orderly panic.

hell. But I don't get to wait for confirmation inside a chemistry lab. So I evacuated. Every time.

To this day (and I am not making this up): four years later, I still get a text message when San Goldilock High School's fire alarm goes off... just to let me know it's another false alarm. Because that's how many times it happened. Because they know I'll want to know. Because I'm basically Pavlov's dog, but instead of drooling, I grab goggles and a clipboard.

Toilet Flush System Technician — "Maintain, troubleshoot, and replace high-pressure commercial toilet systems." Every bathroom in my building was either flooding, out of order, or covered in mysterious sticky footprints. I've personally plunged, shut off valves, left angry work orders, and taught three students how not to flush paper towels. I've also diagnosed leaks faster than the district plumber. Do I need a license or just the trauma?

Elevator Call Center Dispatcher — "Respond calmly and efficiently to elevator entrapment situations." Please. I've coached students through panic attacks, hallway fights, impromptu projectile vomiting and once, when a kid got their head stuck between two chairs, I was able to work with him to avoid a crisis. I can talk anyone through anything, including a student sobbing while the fire alarm blares and another one asks if they can "just eat lunch in here."

Custodial Support Specialist (Level 1) — "Assist in maintaining a clean and safe learning environment." I've cleaned up a student's vomit with a paper towel and a prayer. I've unclogged sinks, swept up glitter, and removed gum from ceiling tiles with a yardstick. My ability to identify smells on contact should be its own certification.

Radio Dispatch Traffic Operator — "Relay clear, real-time updates to coordinate mobile units and emergency teams." During my extremely important tenure as Assistant Principal on Special Assignment at MOTC (that's Maintenance, Operations, Technology, and Construction), I was given one mission every Friday: monitor The Radio.

This wasn't just any radio. This was a walkie-talkie-meets-alien-invasion-alert-system, complete with a giant antenna, a battery the size of a toddler, and the energy of a device that once intercepted Soviet signals. It sat in my office like a bomb I wasn't trained to disarm. Occasionally, without warning, it would screech to life with something like: "Homebase, this is the high school. We are clear."

Who was speaking? Unknown. What were they clear of? Also unknown. Why did it always happen the moment I took a bite of food or opened Outlook? A mystery for the gods.

My only job, my sole contribution to this mysterious surveillance operation, was to run, not walk, across the office and shout into the static: "Copy that."

That was it. No debrief. No follow-up. Just me, responding to phantom voices like I was a dispatch for Area 51.

To this day, I still don't know what I was confirming. But I confirmed it like my pension depended on it. And if I can handle Cold War-grade radio duty with zero training, a vague job description, and the constant fear I was talking over a gas leak call, trust me, I can coordinate anything.

Document Scanner Technician (and Fax Machine Necromancer) — "Digitize and archive sensitive documents with precision and consistency." I once scanned 400 IEPs into a glitchy district database while being interrupted every six minutes by a student asking if "this will be on the test." The scanner jammed every third file. The upload system timed out every tenth. I still made it work, mostly out of spite.

I even named the scanner Janet (as in, "Dammit Janet!"; long live Rocky Horror). We had a bond. She hummed when she was happy and screamed when she wasn't. May she rest in pieces.

And now, in the year 2025, I am regularly told to print a document (in a classroom with no printer, no toner, and zero remaining budget for paper), sign it by hand, and then (I wish I were kidding here) fax it. Yes, fax it to the district. Not scan. Not email. Not uploading. FAX.

You want 21st-century outcomes with 1997 equipment, 1983 protocols and a 1979 budget. I've reverse-engineered broken copiers, extracted jammed documents with a dissecting probe, and begged the front office fax machine to send a page without sounding like it was calling for help in Morse code.

So yeah, I digitize. I archive. I scan. I upload. And I also commune with fax ghosts: ancient, toner-stained phantoms who only appear when the Wi-Fi is down and the moon is full.

Specimen Transport Logistics Clerk — "Ensure biohazard samples are moved in compliance with safety protocols." As a chemistry teacher, what could possibly go wrong? Between flammable liquids, broken glass, and hormones in the air thick enough to ignite on their own, every day was a live experiment in risk management.

But, wait: I wasn't just the chemistry teacher. I was also the science department chair, which meant storing old biohazard materials and previously dissected "specimens" in various questionable refrigerators across campus became my unofficial hobby. Forget cheese: I spent my free time betting on which formaldehyde-soaked organ would survive the weekend with the fewest rat bites. If you've never opened a container on Monday morning only to find what used to be a fetal pig now looks like it lost a turf war to a mouse the size of a chihuahua, you haven't lived.

I transported specimens between classrooms, across parking lots, through rainstorms and fire drills, while carrying Petri dishes, a Ziplock of agar, and a scalpel in my teeth like a biology-themed pirate. I once stopped a student mid-lick from putting their tongue on a dish labeled "DO NOT TOUCH, MOLDY AS HELL." And, yes, every culture survived intact.

Did I have gloves? Sometimes.

A cart? No.

A will to live? That was questionable.

But I followed protocols the best I could, given that most of our storage solutions had been retired by the CDC in 1996. So if you're wondering whether I'm capable of managing biological logistics under pressure, the answer is: Sweetie, I did it with a broken fridge, a class full of high schoolers, and something leaking onto my shoe.

CDC, call me. Or better yet, apologize.

Emergency Communication Protocol Tester — "Simulate response procedures under various emergency scenarios." Let me tell you about the time we practiced a lockdown during a pep rally while a parent was trying to drop off cupcakes. I don't simulate chaos; I lived it.

Inventory Control Auditor, Sharp Object & Chemical Warfare Division — "Track and manage secure inventory in school environments." I once had to count every scissor, scalpel, and dissecting needle in my lab because a student claimed "the frog ate it." I maintained spreadsheets that would make OSHA proud and chased down rogue glass slides like they were contraband. Do you want my audit log or a signed confession?

Oh, and did I mention I was also the school's Chemical Safety Coordinator? Which meant, once a month, I had the distinct honor of taking inventory of every single chemical on campus. Not just mine. Everyone's. There was a district spreadsheet, a masterpiece of merged cells and bureaucratic indifference, that I was expected to update after combing through every science cabinet, closet, and mislabeled jug of "maybe acid."

This fun little side quest? Paid me a generous $600 per year. That's $60 a month. For hours of unsupervised, hazardous, unpaid overtime-adjacent chemical tracking. But hey, who says we do this for the money?

The Ones That Got Away - But Shouldn't Have

If there's one thing teaching has prepared me for, it's applying for jobs I'm overqualified for and still hearing, "We went with another candidate." Translation: "We wanted someone who smiles more, asks fewer questions, and doesn't point out when our 'innovative' ideas are just old ideas in new fonts."

The irony? I've managed more people in a single semester than some "Directors" will in their entire careers. I've navigated budgets, schedules, crises, and parents who think FERPA is a type of pasta. I've done it without an assistant, without overtime, and without a single catered lunch that didn't come in a styrofoam box.

Yet, somehow, when I send in my résumé, it's like applying to be a lifeguard after surviving a shipwreck. You'd think the fact that I kept 180 teenagers alive, engaged, and relatively non-violent for years would count for something.

So here's my final thought: *If you've read this far and you're still not ready to hire me, I hope you enjoy your new hire.* I'm sure they'll do great, once they Google how to mediate a screaming match, re-write a grant proposal, coordinate a field trip, run a fire drill, teach quadratic equations, and file an OSHA report…all before lunch.

Me? I'll be over here, updating my résumé. Again. But hey, I'll just apply to be a barista. I don't qualify for that either, I've never operated a frother under duress, but I do love my coffee.

Things I'd Say at a Job Interview If I Were Allowed to Be Honest

Job interviews are a lot like teaching observations: everyone pretends this is a normal, natural interaction but, deep down, we all know it's an absurd performance. The difference is that, in teaching, you get evaluated on how well you can juggle 37 teenagers per hour and a lesson on photosynthesis and, in an interview, you get evaluated on how convincingly you can say, "I'm a team player" without rolling your eyes.

So, if I were allowed to answer honestly, without the HR-safe filter, here's what I'd really say:

> Q: So tell me about yourself.
>
> A: Sure. I survived 14 years in public education without developing a visible drinking problem, and I'm still legally allowed near teenagers. I consider that a win.
>
> Q: What are your strengths?
>
> A: I can de-escalate a fight, write a 3-page sub plan in my sleep, and teach mitosis while a fire alarm is going off and a parent is emailing me about why their son should get credit for "trying." Also, I have an iron bladder and the ability to cry silently during lunch.
>
> Q: How do you handle pressure?
>
> A: I once taught during an active shooter lockdown while someone in the back of the room was making a shiv out of a broken ruler. I'm fine.

Q: Tell me about a challenge you faced.

A: You mean besides being expected to function as a therapist, tutor, nurse, life coach, security guard, data analyst, and social worker, for $60k and a bag of stale Funyuns during Teacher Appreciation Week?

Q: Why are you leaving education?

A: Because I want to live.

Q: Why did you leave your last role?

A: Because of my mental health, dignity, and ability to digest food without acid reflux. Also, I realized "making a difference" doesn't require self-demoralization.

Q: What would your previous coworkers say about you?

A: They'd say I'm dependable, supportive, and unnervingly calm for someone who taught an entire semester with a bullet hole in the classroom window. When I asked the principal to replace it, she told me it gave me "street credibility." So I told my students, "Ignore the ballistics evidence and balance your chemical equations, not the crime scene."

Q: Tell us about a time you demonstrated leadership.

A: That would be the time I mediated a screaming match between two 10th graders, while redirecting 35 other students, during a fire drill, with the assistant principal watching. Also, I once managed a department meeting without stabbing anyone. That counts.

Q: What's your biggest weakness?

A: I care too much. And also, my fight-or-flight response is permanently activated by the sound of a school bell. Like, I hear one at Target and suddenly I'm scanning for hall passes and emotionally bracing for a vape cloud and a passive-aggressive email.

Q. How do you handle stress?

A: I used to cry in my car, scream into the steering wheel,

and walk back in like I wasn't silently begging the universe to take me out via rogue fire drill.

Now? I take magnesium like it's Xanax, drink tea like it's vodka, and update my résumé every time someone says "new initiative."

Q: What makes you a good fit for this position?

A: Because I already know how to do 75% of this job, and I'll figure out the other 25% before you finish onboarding. Also? I will never ask for help unless it's urgent; I'm a teacher. We don't die, we improvise.

The truth is, teaching was the most high-stakes, multi-hat, improvisational role I'll ever play. I didn't just teach; I managed crises, diffused chaos, negotiated peace treaties, ran on zero resources, and still hit my deadlines. If I can survive public education, trust me; your quarterly reports don't scare me.

So there you have it—my teaching résumé.

Look, I know what you're thinking: "This person sounds unhinged." And you're not wrong. But here's the thing: I'm functionally unhinged which, in the teaching world, is a superpower. I can juggle a mental breakdown, a parent complaint, and a lesson on photosynthesis simultaneously while maintaining eye contact and remembering everyone's pronouns.

I've been forged in the fires of standardized testing, tempered by the tears of budget cuts, and polished to a gleaming shine by the daily realization that society expects me to raise other people's children while barely being able to afford my own groceries.

I'm like a Swiss Army knife, if Swiss Army knives came with PTSD and an unhealthy relationship with coffee.

After 14 years of this beautiful disaster, I've developed skills most people only dream of. I can sense drama from three hallways away, negotiate peace treaties between hormonal teenagers, and teach complex scientific concepts while simultaneously preventing someone from eating glue. I've got the patience of a saint, the reflexes of a ninja, and the emotional regulation of someone who's been through intensive therapy (because I have).

So yes, I'm leaving education. But I'm not running away, I'm strategically retreating with a skill set that would make Navy SEALs weep with envy. Any employer lucky enough to hire me is getting someone who's been battle-tested in the trenches of public education and lived to tell the tale.

Plus, I promise I won't cry in your supply closet. Much.

And here's the thing about surviving: It doesn't mean I came out unscathed. It means I learned how to keep smiling while I bled, and eventually, I started to wonder how much of myself I would be willing to leave behind just to keep going.

YOU CAN'T FIX THE SYSTEM
IF YOU'RE THE SACRIFICE.

You Can't Fix the System If You're the Sacrifice — They'll Gladly Let You Die for the Cause, Then Replace You by Monday

Here's the thing about being "one of the good ones" in education: They will cheer you on right up until you collapse, and then they'll quietly step over your body to hand your classroom keys to the next idealist.

There was a time when I wore my exhaustion like an honor. First one in. Last one out. Lunch at my desk. Tutoring after school. I was "one of the good ones," and the system loved that. They love it when you break yourself for the mission. They love it when you do the work of three people and don't ask for more. They love it when you say 'yes', say 'thank you', say 'it's fine', even when it's not.

But the truth is? You don't fix a broken system by dying inside it.

Take this past year. As a Community Day School teacher, I realized I was teaching 22 classes. At the same time. No, that's not a typo. That's real.

My fourth-period class alone included:
- High School Health
- Middle School Health
- Biology A
- Chemistry B
- Spanish 1
- Interactions A (whatever that is this week)

Six subjects. One classroom. One teacher. No curriculum.

It was an academic Thunderdome, and I was the only one holding the clipboard.

Then came my evaluation. The assistant principal observed the chaos and, with a straight face, told me "there was no direct instruction."

You don't say. I, a 14-year veteran teacher with a Master's in Education, an MS in Educational Leadership, and a Doctorate in Education, had somehow failed to deliver a high-quality lecture to six subjects simultaneously in a single 55-minute block.

I told him, "I couldn't find a single standard that tied all these subjects together. If you know of one, I'd love to see how you'd model that." He blinked and said, "It's your job to know what to teach."

Ah. Of course. Silly me.

Because in this system, it's always my fault.

When the resources don't exist? That's my fault.

When the structure is broken? That's my fault.

When you're set up to fail and don't pull off a miracle? That's my fault.

Because this system wasn't designed to support you. It was designed to use you. And every time you stay late, skip lunch, say "yes" when you mean "help," it feeds the illusion that this is sustainable. That teachers can do anything. That they'll always figure it out.

But: Just because you can, doesn't mean you should.

You are not the emergency plan. You are not a patch. You are not the fix. And you are not responsible for holding up a structure that was rotting before you got there. And if the building collapses the second you walk away? That's not your legacy. That's proof it was never safe to begin with.

 A Note to Policy Makers:

I know there is a waiting list of people begging to enter the teaching career (that was said with sarcasm), but imagine what would happen if teachers only taught what they are credentialed in, compensated for all additional work including tutoring, extra prep, IEP analysis. Then: maybe, *just maybe*, it would be worth my time.

PARENTS

BLAME

KIDS

ADMIN

TESTS

EMAILS

POLICYMAKERS

by Dr Dana

STILL SMILING...

MARRIED TO THE TEACHING CAREER
THAT NEVER LOVED ME BACK.

GRIEVING THE CAREER YOU THOUGHT YOU HAD, BUT IT NEVER LOVED YOU BACK

You don't just walk away from a career like this. You drag yourself, bleeding, carrying the weight of a thousand unpaid hours and a lifetime of "but I thought we were making a difference." You grieve it like a bad relationship, the kind you swore was "the one" while ignoring all the red flags stapled to the staff lounge bulletin board.

There's this story, maybe you've heard it, about a quirky, faithful woman stuck in a flood. She's a bit eccentric, loves long walks on the beach, is a romantic at heart, a pragmatic nerd by day, and she labels her Tupperware. Water's creeping in. A neighbor paddles by in a boat: "Hop in!" She waves him off. "No, thanks. God will save me." The water climbs higher. A helicopter shows up and drops a ladder: "Grab on!" She smiles politely. "No, thanks. God will save me."

Then, the chef's kiss — a devastatingly attractive man flies by in a tiny plane. Cowboy hat, aviator glasses and the kind of smile that makes you forget your own name. He tosses her a harness and says, "I'll take you to safety." She fluffs her curls, pretends her heart isn't racing, and shouts back, "I'm good! God's got this!"

She drowns. Soaked socks, the whole thing.

She gets to heaven, very soggy and very annoyed, and says to God: "I thought you were going to save me." And God, clearly done with her, says, "I sent you a boat, a helicopter, and a hot guy in a plane wearing a cowboy hat. What else did you want—a glitter-covered PowerPoint?"

This summer, I realized something. **That woman was me.**

Except, instead of drowning in water, I was drowning in district initiatives, unpaid hours, and secondhand Expo fumes. I saw the signs. The boat? The migraines. The helicopter? My magician friend, currently getting paid to make cool effects for TV while I was still figuring out how to make the copy machine work without jamming. The plane? That time I blacked out in my car because I couldn't face walking into one more meeting about "vertical alignment."

And still, I stayed. "I'll just push through! It'll get better! I'll survive on caffeine and blind optimism!" No, babe. You're not built for martyrdom. You're built for more.

So finally, I said it: I'm not drowning for this job. Not dying in this classroom. Not giving one more ounce of my sanity to a system that thinks a jeans pass is a reward.

No one tells you that leaving teaching is like breaking up with the love of your life, except the love of your life was a gaslighting, emotionally unavailable dumpster fire that occasionally gave you donuts and called it support.

You thought you'd retire in that classroom. You thought you'd have alumni come back to thank you in slow-motion montages with soft piano music playing in the background. You thought the testing, chaos, and politics would settle if you just hung on long enough. You thought someone would step in.

They didn't. But you did. And now? You're out. Not because you didn't care, but because caring was killing you.

And still… you miss it. You miss the good days. The random kid who said thank you. The lesson that worked. The weird joy of convincing a 15-year-old that the periodic table actually matters. You miss the rhythm, the year that had structure, even if that structure was held together with duct tape, caffeine, and unprocessed trauma. You almost miss the copier. (Let's not get carried away.)

Because here's the truth no one prints on a t-shirt: You didn't just lose a job. You lost an identity. You weren't teaching. You were a teacher. And when that title disappears? You're left staring into the void like, What was it all for? Who am I now? Do I still get the teacher discount at Michaels?

Grief sneaks up on you. At Target, when you pass the school supplies and instinctively start calculating how much of your own money you can blow before the first paycheck hits. At 7:59 AM, when your body jolts because the bell should be ringing. When you realize you don't need to buy nameplates or buy-in anymore, and you feel guilty for not missing it more.

But here's the thing: You didn't quit because you couldn't handle it. You left because you handled it far too well for far too long.

You outgrew a job that expected you to be a therapist, data analyst, parent whisperer, tech wizard, janitor, and motivational speaker, all while being underpaid and publicly blamed for everything from national test scores to a kid's bad attitude. You mourned the version of teaching that lived in your heart, the Hallmark version, the Hollywood-scripted cafeteria miracle and the "standing on desks and quoting poetry" nonsense.

But that version? It never existed. It was built on idealism and the lie that passion can replace protection, that love can outwork a broken system.

So go ahead. Grieve. Cry. Scream. Buy overpriced candles and call it healing. Lie on the floor and listen to your "dramatic rebirth" playlist. Write an email to your former principal in your Notes app, then delete it. (Or don't. I'm not your boss.)

But then? Let it go.

Because you're not weak. You're not selfish. You're not a traitor to the profession. You're a survivor of it. And now, it's your turn to be rescued, by the life you were meant to have.

So when that boat shows up? Get in.

When the helicopter drops the ladder? Climb.

And when the hot guy in the plane circles back around—cowboy hat, aviators, and all? Grab the damn harness. And hold on.

Because sometimes the smartest move is to stop clinging to the sinking ship, embrace the fantasy, and as the kids say, save the horse and ride the cowboy. The next chapter is already waiting. And this time? It chooses you back.

Even death doesn't solve the staffing shortage.

This Time,
It's About Me, Not the
District's Staffing Shortage

For the first time in a long time, I'm not standing in a classroom wondering if the silence means peace or if someone finally succeeded in pulling the fire alarm and lighting a trash can on fire. I'm not scavenging for pencils like a raccoon with a master's degree or begging IT for a third loaner Chromebook. I'm not preparing for Back-to-School Night with a smile that says "Of course I'm happy to explain the grading policy again" while mentally calculating how long I can survive on caffeine and spite. I'm not trying to figure out how thirty-eight students are supposed to share twelve pairs of lab goggles without passing around Pink Eye like it's extra credit.

I'm not planning a classroom. I'm planning an escape.

Because the truth is, I've spent years being "useful." "Flexible." A "team player." The person who says 'yes' when everyone else runs. "Useful" is just a nice way to say "disposable." And, for a long time, I wore that like a badge. I even had one of those workplace safety signs. You know, the ones that say "___ Days Since Last Injury?" Mine said, "___ Days Since Calling Child Protective Service (CPS), Police, or Ambulance." I never made it past five. That number resets constantly.

One day, I'd be sending five kids to the nurse's office after discovering their "Cinnamon Toast Crunch" was actually Cannabis Toast Crunch. (Fun fact: distinguishing cinnamon from cannabis wasn't covered in my credential program.) Two days later, I'd be making a mandated report about a bruise no one else noticed. Zero days later, when the campus went into lockdown, I had to pretend it was a drill so the freshmen wouldn't start crying (again).

Reset. Reset. Reset. And the system never blinked.

Then there was Valerie. She was quiet. Brilliant. The kind of kid who slips between the cracks so smoothly you almost don't notice she's bleeding. She used to ditch school for nine days straight and then show up on the tenth just to avoid the automated call home. But she could draw. My god, she could draw. So I told her, "Why don't you just come to my art class every day for one week?" And she did. Then she started showing up in fifth period, not her assigned class, just to sit quietly in my room and draw. Then she'd stay for sixth, our actual art period. I thought maybe we were turning a corner. That maybe showing up for art meant she'd start showing up for herself.

Then, on a Friday, she killed herself.

We didn't get a memo. No official word. No warning. Just a hallway whisper on Monday morning: "Did you hear about Valerie?" We got confirmation on Tuesday and were told to keep quiet until the district figured out how to respond. No announcement. No letter to students. No moment of silence. Just business as usual.

The following Tuesday (yes, you read that right: the following Tuesday, eight days after we found out and ten days after she killed herself), they brought in a grief counselor. For the staff. At the staff meeting. We sat in tiny plastic chairs and were told we could "process in private if needed" while the students, the ones who sat next to her, laughed with her, asked if she was okay, were given nothing. Not even acknowledgment that she was gone.

I sat next to the guidance counselor that day, just before the meeting started. I turned to her and said, "I was going to send Valerie to see you today. But then I remembered, she's not coming back." She looked at me, stunned. And I didn't stop.

"If we had talked about Valerie in these staff meetings instead of just reviewing social-emotional guidelines, maybe she'd still be alive. Maybe we should spend this staff meeting talking about our living kids."

I don't regret saying it. I regret that it had to be said at all.

That's what I'm walking away from. Not the kids. Never the kids. I'm walking away from the silence. From the gaslighting. From the kind of system that asks you to bleed out quietly and still smile for the district newsletter.

I don't know what comes next for me, but I know it won't involve pretending that surviving a broken system is noble. It won't be answering late-night emails from administrators who never set foot in my classroom. It won't be another year of wondering which student I'll lose next and whether I'll be allowed to say their name out loud. What's next might be perfroming magic. Might be writing. Might be sleeping in and remembering what it feels like to exist without a bell dictating my every move.

I don't know exactly what I'll do, but I know I'll choose it. It won't be assigned to me. It won't be forced, guilted, or sugar-coated. It won't start with "can you just" and end with me sacrificing my sanity for a staff meeting that could've been an email.

I have skills. Real ones. The kind you earn when you're teaching during a lockdown, managing a fistfight, and re-writing lesson plans because the Internet went out, all before second period. I've mediated, de-escalated, parented, translated, taught, and survived. I've led with patience I didn't know I had and fire I wasn't supposed to show. I've buried students. I've called CPS and 911 and parents who never should've had custody. I've cried in parking lots and walked back inside anyway.

I don't owe the system another breath. I've given it brilliance, blood, and every last piece of myself. I showed up for everyone else. Now, I show up for myself.

No more permission slips. No more drowning quietly in floodwaters I was never meant to survive. No more pretending not to see the lifeboats because I was too busy patching holes in someone else's. I'm walking toward a life I didn't think I was allowed to want.

And for the first time in years, I'm not just surviving.

I'm free.

If You Truly Respect Teachers, You'll Give Me the 4:30 Appointment

Because Caffeine Won't Save Me From a Root Canal.

If you're not an educator but you say you respect teachers, this chapter is for you. Not because we need your validation, but because respect is a verb, not a sentiment.

So let's break it down. If you truly respect educators, you'll change how you operate around us. Not with empty gestures, not with Pinterest apples, but with real-life accommodations that actually reflect the reality of our jobs.

Let's start here: If you are a tailor, doctor, therapist, dentist, notary, car mechanic, or anyone else who books appointments… you will block out 4:30 PM exclusively for teachers.

Yes. I said it.

Four-thirty is the Teacher Hour. You will hold that spot like it's sacred. Because teachers can't just leave work at 2:00 like everyone thinks. We're not done at 3:00, either. We're often still supervising, tutoring, emailing, meeting, grading, and trying to remember what breathing feels like.

We can't sneak away for a "quick appointment" during the day because:
- We probably can't get a sub. Subs are rare. Subs for science teachers? Unicorns. And when there's no sub, our coworkers have to cover for us during their own prep time, meaning we're stealing someone else's oxygen just to get a throat swab.

- It's easier to show up half-dead than write a sub plan. If I have to write five pages of emergency instructions, find backup materials, leave color-coded notes, and pre-print copies so someone can come in, take attendance wrong, and show a video the kids will ignore... it's not worth it.

- My principal finally scheduled a meeting with me. The one I've been begging for since February. The one where he might finally approve of the field trip my students have spent all year preparing for, the one where they'll actually see the real-world application of everything I've been teaching them. And if I miss that window? It's gone. Because he didn't reply to 12 emails, but suddenly I have 20 minutes today, during 3rd period, when I was supposed to take sick leave. So I stayed.

- My doctor never called back anyway. So I'd burn a sick day to do... nothing. No prescription. No answers. No appointment. And now I've wasted one of the ten sick days I get per year.

Ten sick days that aren't only for when I get sick. That's for when my kid gets sick, emergencies, dental work, biopsies, blood work, funerals, the flu, food poisoning, mental breakdowns, and unavoidable life. And yes, that includes the day the toilet overflows, the electrician needs to fix a breaker so my microwave won't kill my A/C, or the water heater replacement that's been "scheduled" for two months.

So yeah—if you truly respect teachers? Give us the damn 4:30 appointment. We'll take it. We'll thank you. We might cry.

And while we're at it:

Don't roll your eyes if we ask for help at Office Depot.

Don't act surprised when we show up looking exhausted—we are.

Don't tell us, "At least you get summers off."

And please don't say, "You're a teacher? God bless you," then vote for people who defund our classrooms and criminalize our work.

If you really respect educators, you'll make space for us, in your schedules, in your business hours, in your systems. Not just during Teacher Appreciation Week.

And if that 4:30 appointment happens to be with a hot dentist in a cowboy hat? Even better. Because sometimes respect looks like letting the teacher leave on time, and sometimes it looks like handing her the damn harness.

Death by PowerPoint: 187 slides later.

Breaking news: homework found alive
and well in the wilds of imagination.

Things We Wish We Could Say at Back-to-School Night (High School Edition)

Welcome to Back-to-School Night, otherwise known as "America's Got Excuses." I'm so glad you took time out of your busy evening to ignore everything I'm about to say while you stare at your phone and pretend your child isn't failing three classes. I've been looking forward to tonight all week, nothing like being blamed for your child's GPA in person instead of over email. They say it takes a village to raise a child. I'd just like to know why the village keeps forwarding its complaints to me.

Here's what we'd love, love to say, if we could drop the polite act and speak from the soul:

- Your kid's not "bad at math"; he's just allergic to effort. Let's call it what it is. He's not confused; he's lazy. He has a calculator in his pocket and still refuses to show work. That's not a learning issue. That's a parenting issue.

- Schoology exists. Use it. Please don't email me asking, "How is she doing in class?" You have the same access I do. If you can log into Amazon and track a package from China, you can click the Grades tab.

- If your child says they turned something in and it's not in the gradebook, they're lying. They didn't submit it. They "forgot." They printed it and left it in the car, on the kitchen table, or possibly in the sediment layer between two ancient geologic epochs.

Look, I'm not gaslighting your child. I've got 160 students, three lab preps, and a to-do list that's now self-aware. I'm not running a controlled experiment on the molecular decay rate of missing essays. Your kid's lab report didn't sublimate, transmute, or slip through a wormhole on its way to my inbox.

If it's not there, it's not there. This isn't quantum mechanics—the assignment doesn't exist in both a graded and ungraded state depending on who's asking. I grade what's there. I document what's missing. I don't have the time, energy, or federal funding to launch an investigation into the Disappearance of an Eleventh Grader's Chemistry Lab Report.

So unless that paper is carbon-dated, spectroscopically verified, and hand-delivered by a neutrino traveling faster than light, we're going to go with: It Wasn't Turned In.

- No, I don't "hate" your child. I'm just done pretending his behavior is normal. Your son told me to "chill" when I asked him to put away his vape. In the middle of class. While exhaling fruit punch-scented rebellion into the air.

Let's be clear: I'm not being dramatic, I'm being restrained. Frankly, I'm showing the kind of composure NASA would study. I'm not sure why I'm the villain here. Why are you yelling at me instead of asking why your underage child is carrying a vape on school grounds (which, fun fact, is a federal violation)? Why are you not checking his backpack? Why is your anger pointed at the person enforcing the law, instead of the minor breaking it?

Spoiler: I don't hate your kid. I hate having to explain basic boundaries while dodging plumes of mango mist and moral whiplash. I'm not out to get him. I'm just not paid enough to pretend this is okay.

- There are 38 kids in six periods. I can't respond to every single email within two hours. I love that you're "just checking in."

Truly. It warms my heart between grading lab reports, writing IEP notes, eating a string cheese for lunch, and crying in my car like a functioning adult.

But here's an idea: Before sending me a fourth message asking why your child has a missing assignment, maybe… I don't know… log in to Schoology. Or Google Classroom. Or whatever platform we've been using for 10 months that I know you have access to, because you used it once to ask about extra credit. Or, radical thought, ask your child. Have an actual conversation. Try parenting.

I get it; it's hard. I have parents, too. They're annoying. But I'd still take mine over you as the chief conspiracy theorist, because at least they wouldn't assume I'm plotting academic sabotage when their kid just didn't click "Submit."

Your child isn't turning in work. They also read at a level that makes me wonder if we need to call a paleontologist instead of a counselor. But I'm still here: showing up, scaffolding, encouraging, and attempting to guide them toward a diploma and a future that ideally includes both health insurance and basic civic awareness. So while you're "just checking in," I'm just trying to keep your kid from becoming the next headline. You're welcome.

- Please stop asking if there's "extra credit." There's regular credit; start there. Your child has turned in 3 out of 18 assignments. At this point, extra credit is like putting frosting on a trash fire.

- Group projects aren't unfair. Life is unfair.

Your kid will absolutely, 100%, without a doubt, have to work with idiots in adulthood. Consider this group project 'future career prep' for your kid. And, no, I will not rearrange the groups because "she always ends up doing all the work." Let her learn boundaries. Let her learn delegation and that sometimes, in life, you get stuck with a Chad and a Brittany who think oxygen is optional and deadlines are theoretical.

You want to take action? Here's a fun idea: Why don't you call the parents of the other group members and tell them how disappointed you are in their children? I'm sure that will foster a beautiful, collaborative learning community grounded in trust, passive aggression, and multi-generational resentment. Group work isn't broken. The world is broken. And your child still has to live in it.

You're welcome for the realism life throws our way. Consider it an unpaid internship in disappointment.

- If your kid is failing three classes and you "had no idea," I don't know what to tell you. He's been grounded from the PlayStation, but not from Snapchat? Let's be honest: he's grounded from consequences, not screens. And, before you email me like the head of the grievance department you are: no, I'm not secretly plotting with the Math and English teachers to tank his GPA. He's doing that all by himself.

- Your child will not be Valedictorian just because you want it. He's not going to Stanford with a 1.7 GPA, a vape pen, and a weekly attendance rate of 63%. Stop calling counselors like we can wave a magic admissions wand. Start setting expectations or at least start Googling 'community college.'

- If you're here just to be seen: Mission Accomplished. You can go now. I see you. You came in full makeup, filmed half my talk for your Facebook reel, nodded like you cared, and left before asking your child what period they have me. That's fine. But let's not pretend it's "involvement." You're here for optics, not outcomes, and trust me, the kids can tell.

And finally: I care. Despite everything, the broken system, the disrespect, the unpaid hours, the absurd demands, I care. I show up. I teach. I grade. I laugh. I cry. And I was still there.

But please understand: I'm here for your child. Not to cover for your parenting. Not to be your punching bag when he fails. And definitely not to star in the conspiracy theory where I personally ruin his life because he didn't turn in his homework.

by Dr Dana

HOW WE CAN FIX THE SCHOOLS

We don't need more funding. We need smarter funding, stronger accountability, and common sense. Everyone's got ideas for fixing education, and most of them start with "we just need more money." But let's be honest: schools are spending like they've got Monopoly money and zero adult supervision.

THE CATCH-UP CIRCUS

Guess who gets to make up the difference when Jacob disappears for two weeks? Not Jacob. *Me*! I get to reprint assignments. Re-explain labs. Grade late work. Give extensions. Stay after school. Field emails from shocked and outraged parents, shocked that their child is failing.

"Well, he didn't know what to do…" Right. Because he was watching fireworks over Sleeping Beauty's castle while we were covering balancing equations.

If school is going to be treated like a pay-per-use service, then let's go all in. Miss 10 days? Here's your invoice for the Annual Daily Attendance (ADA) we lost. Request tutoring? That's an hourly fee. Need make-up quizzes, labs, and personal re-teaching? I'll send you an estimate. Want to challenge the F they earned after not showing up for three weeks? Submit a customer service ticket. Response time: 30 days if the paperwork is filled out correctly. (If not, please edit your paperwork and re-submit…)

If you skipped class at a community college, you'd still pay tuition. If you missed work for two weeks without calling, you'd get fired. But in K–12, we're supposed to welcome your kid back like nothing happened, with a smile, a flexible return policy, and maybe even a sticker.

Access means nothing if students don't show up. And when they do, Starbucks in hand, asking if we're "doing anything today," we're supposed to act like they're victims of an unfair system. No. They are products of a system that refuses to hold anyone accountable including their parents, or lack thereof!

If I ran the district, absences would equal mandatory parent service hours. Make copies. Clean the lunch area. Water the roses that haven't died yet. Or sit next to your kid until they're caught up. Absences would mean a bill for lost ADA. And, if you want after-hours help: book a slot, bring me coffee, and pay my hourly overtime rate.

Attendance matters. It affects learning, funding, and everything teachers try to build in a classroom. Until we treat absenteeism like the disaster it is, we'll keep bleeding resources on kids who treat school like a side quest.

Step right up to the greatest show on Earth; also known as teaching.

THANKS FOR THE TECH EQUITY. IT'S DOING WONDERS.

When those kids finally come back, they often show up empty-handed. No Chromebook. No charger. Maybe no backpack. "It's broken" or "I lost it" is the only explanation, said with the same energy you'd use to mention you forgot to buy bread.

Then it's a trip to the tech office, where repair costs and replacement fees don't exist because that would be "inequitable." We've built a system where care and accountability are optional. One student smashes their Chromebook into a locker and gets a new one without a question. Another treats theirs like it's a rare collector's item and gets nothing extra, except resentment.

Meanwhile, I'm not allowed to have a class set of Chromebooks, because that would make too much sense. So when a student shows up without one, I'm supposed to just "adjust" the plan. Some teachers print paper copies. Others rotate devices like musical chairs. I manage my rage while the kid who hasn't submitted anything in three weeks shrugs and says, "It's not my fault." And technically, they're right. Because we've told them again and again: you are not responsible for the tools we gave you.

We're not building digital literacy. We're building entitlement. We're teaching kids that if you break your tools, someone else replaces them. No cost. No accountability. No concept of value.

If I ran the system, every student would sign a Chromebook Agreement with three rules:

1. You break it, you pay for it. Full price.
2. Lose it twice, and your parents or guardians cover it.
3. Can't handle the tech? You don't default to paper like it's 2003.

Once value is attached, miraculous things happen. Backpacks grow compartments. Chargers stop being "left at home." Devices stop doubling as frisbees.

Until then, I'll be over here teaching 21st-century skills with a 20th-century photocopier, while another kid scrolls TikTok on their fully charged personal iPhone and tells me their district Chromebook "doesn't work."

"FREE" BREAKFAST AND LUNCH IS NOT FREE, AND IS NOT WANTED

Feeding kids sounds noble. Nobody wants a child to go hungry. But, what good is feeding them food they will not eat? Walk through a school cafeteria and you'll see unopened milk cartons, soggy pizza, and bruised apples filling trash cans faster than stomachs.

We are spending millions on meals that end up in dumpsters. Here's an idea: Partner with local restaurants. Let kids scan a QR code for a taco truck. Keep the food hot, the flavor real, and the waste minimal. Right now, we are running a taxpayer-funded food disposal program with a side of ant infestation.

Students march through a government-mandated buffet and must take a milk they didn't ask for, a "fruit" or "vegetable" that's either frozen solid or mushy enough to count as baby food, and a main dish sealed in more plastic than a barbie doll impersonator at a red-carpet event. By the time they hit the trash can stationed by the exit, the milk and fruit are gone. The entrée might get opened. Or not. Either way, the landfill wins.

Nutrition, by way of landfill.

Then there's breakfast in the classroom. Every morning, a lucky child retrieves the "wheelie" breakfast cart, and I track who took what for federal paperwork. The counts never match. I have marked everyone as "fed" just to avoid another passive-aggressive note in my mailbox. Leftovers rot in a science classroom where food isn't allowed, attracting ants who are extra grateful for the program.

Kids don't want USDA ham squares. They want tacos, ramen, or something that doesn't taste like cardboard. Meanwhile, half of them stroll in with a $15 Starbucks drink and $100 manicures, proving they are not teetering on the edge of famine.

And let's talk about the student-run black market. Chips are currency. Hot Cheetos are stock options. Kids trade breakfast burritos for Pokémon cards and vape hits. It's not a cafeteria. It's Rikers with less security.

This is not about health. It is about optics. We put on a show of feeding kids, but when the curtain falls, all that's left is spoiled milk, resentment, and thousands in rotting federal funding. We are not feeding bellies or minds. We are feeding a bureaucracy. And it's the only thing in the building with an appetite.

WHAT ACCOUNTABILITY COULD LOOK LIKE

We're running schools like charities, not institutions of learning. We're so scared of being "unfair" that we forget to be effective.

You want equity? Start by teaching that actions have consequences: for students, for families, for everyone in the system. Schools don't need more programs; they need enforcement. We don't need more initiatives; we need follow-through. Stop measuring success by how many Chromebooks we pass out, and start measuring by how many come back.

If you ever want to see what it looks like when a school district panics but doesn't want to actually fix anything, just wait for them to roll out a new after-school program. These things are the educational equivalent of a glitter bomb: flashy, chaotic and, once the dust settles, utterly useless.

"Enrichment" has been watered down to coloring geometric shapes to lo-fi beats or "Mindful Movement," which is just unsupervised stretching in a multi-purpose room while the janitor vacuums. Summer school, once a serious opportunity to catch up, has been reduced to Worksheet Island: a sad little packet, a login to Edgenuity, and a clock ticking toward lunch. The kids who need it most? They're at Disneyland, in another country, or just vanished.

THE DISTRICT'S CRISIS PLAYBOOK GOES LIKE THIS:

Step 1: Host a meeting.
Step 2: Unveil a program with a catchy acronym.
Step 3: Slap "equity" or "resilience" on the branding.
Step 4: Make it mandatory.
Step 5: Collect no data.
Step 6: Look confused when nothing changes.

We've had "grit" curricula, "growth mindset" assemblies, trauma-informed yoga, SEL circles, peer mediation workshops, and—my personal favorite—silent reflection stations. Meanwhile, our science textbooks predate the iPhone, our copier is permanently jammed, and we don't have basic supplies. But sure, let's hand out glitter pens so kids can journal their way to success.

Then comes Wellness Week—the week we get flavored water and "positive self-talk" posters while the district also schedules six IEPs, a PD session, and asks if we can cover for a missing sub during our prep. And if you object? Someone will kindly remind you to "reframe your mindset" and invite you to a self-care Zoom scheduled during your only bathroom break.

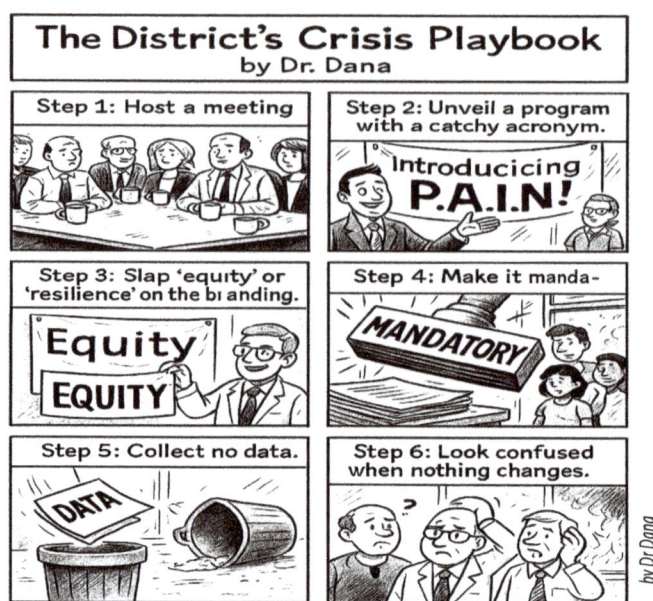

We don't need another after-school "Resilience Through Poetry" club that three kids attend and no one supervises. We need structure. We need consequences. We need policies that don't vanish the moment a parent complains on Facebook.

We've created a system addicted to distractions, constantly launching new initiatives so no one has to admit the last twenty failed. "We tried nothing, and we're all out of ideas" should be printed on every district mission statement.

Until we stop throwing glitter at gaping wounds and calling it innovation, we'll keep spinning our wheels in the same broken machine. And all we'll have to show for it is another unopened milk carton, another missing Chromebook, and another Jacob who didn't show up—again.

TEACHERS AREN'T THE FLAW

If you've made it to the end, you might think this book was a rant. That I sat down to complain about bad lunches, broken Chromebooks, endless meetings, and all the little absurdities that make teaching feel like performance art in a broken theater. But it's not just that.

It's about the fact that these problems are fixable, and we're just not fixing them. We keep telling teachers to "be resilient," when what we need is a system that doesn't run on burning people out. We hand out yoga mats instead of planning time, pizza coupons instead of pay raises, and mood journals instead of soap in the bathrooms. None of this requires a miracle. It requires priorities.

The truth is, society doesn't need to worship teachers. We don't need parades, or mugs, or hashtags. What we need is for everyone—parents, policymakers, the public—to work with us instead of around us. That means:

- Holding students (and their families) accountable for showing up, prepared to learn.
- Funding the basics before the extras: paper before programs, planning time before PR stunts.
- Listening to teachers before you spend money "for" them. We'll tell you exactly what works, if you'd just ask.
- Stop pretending that schools can single-handedly fix every social problem. We are educators, not substitute parents, social workers, tech support, and nutritionists all rolled into one.

Because here's the truth: teachers want to teach. We want to do the job we trained for. We want to see kids succeed, grow, and surprise us in ways that make all the hard parts worth it. But we can't keep doing it alone, and we shouldn't have to.

This is not about "saving" teachers. It's about saving public education from death by a thousand paper cuts. Every broken copier, every useless program, every unreturned Chromebook, every parent email written in rage instead of partnership: it all adds up. And if we keep ignoring it? It won't just be teachers walking away. It'll be the whole promise of what a public school is supposed to be.

So let's stop with the stickers, the slogans, and the empty gestures. We don't need you to cheer louder. We need you to pick up a bucket and help bail out the boat. You keep asking, "How can we fix education?" Try this instead: "How can we stop enabling dysfunction and start modeling the real world?"

You don't need to spend more money. You need to spend it like it matters. You need to stop treating Chromebooks like disposable party favors, stop calling coloring pages "enrichment," and stop pretending that being "welcoming" means never enforcing a rule. Because right now, here's the truth no one puts in the board packet, that we are the only industry expected to function without accountability. We hand out free tools, free food, free second chances and, when they're wasted, broken, or ignored, we reward the same behavior again. And for what? So that Jacob, fresh from his third trip to Disneyland this semester, can roll into class in pajama pants, shrug off two weeks of missed work, and ask, "Did I miss anything?" Yes, Jacob. You missed everything. And the best part? You'll get it all handed back to you anyway.

But hey, don't worry. I get the summers off.

Multiplying Problems

by Dr Dana

IF YOU TEACH

If you teach, speak loud,
    project through the crowd,
    write it all down,
    make your paperwork proud.
Hand this book quick
    to that clueless friend,
    who chirps, "You're fine,
    it's not bad, it'll end!"
Quit saying you're sorry
    for asking fair pay,
    or skipping the chant of
    "Namaste."
You're not wrong, not a pest,
    to demand some respect,
    not just a mug
    the district collects.
You want protection? Support?
    Not applause on a stage.
    Those raises mean nothing,
    send a massage entourage.
You want training that's useful,
    not nonsense on screens,
    not "Breathing Through Stress"
    with stale tangerines.
Stop covering classes
    for free on your prep,
    while homework multiplies
    like rabbits in a mess.
Take back your lunch—
    the whole thirty bite,
    don't swap it for duty,
    or meetings at night.
Say no to the weekends,
    to "volunteer" shows,
    your time isn't free,
    it's not how it goes.
This job takes your heart,
    your wit, and your spine—
    don't sell it for cupcakes
    and headlines that shine.

The system is broken,
    it's cracked, it's askew,
    you're not over-dramatic—
    you're seeing what's true.
So teach with your wit,
    your sarcasm loud,
    but guard what is yours,
    don't bow to the crowd.
'Cause if you don't fight
    for the time that you need,
    they'll hand you a whistle—
    and call it "Lead."

Excuses: Family-Owned and Operated

IF YOU PARENT

If you parent, ask questions that matter,
    not "Why's there no glue?"
    (We bought 400 sticks,
    ask your kid what they do.)
Support your teachers
    with more than cake,
    We're drowning in frosting,
    a chair would be great.
Teach your child
    that respect's not a perk,
    And no, the teacher's not
    "just being a jerk."
If your instinct is rage,
    take a breath, take a lap,
    Then maybe don't send
    that all-caps parent trap.
Don't storm the office
    with secondhand tales,
    Your kid may be charming,
    but trust me, they fail.
We need you to parent,
    not play their best friend,
    Because childhood's short,
    but the bills never end.
We're here to support you,
    not raise them alone,
    So set some boundaries
    before they've all grown.
If they're failing?
    It's not just "my style" to blame.
    School is a team sport;
    we're all in the game.
When you side with your kid
    no matter the facts,
    They learn that excuses
    can cover the cracks.

Teach them that homework
    is theirs to complete,
    And showing up matters;
    it's not just a seat.
So partner with us,
    don't fight every call,
    We want them to thrive,
    but we can't do it all.
Because the truth is this:
    when parents engage,
    It changes the story,
    it turns the page.
And when your kid grows
    and their schooling is done,
    You'll know you raised
    someone ready to run.
So be the backbone,
    the guide, the one who holds
    steady,
    Because the world they're
    heading into?
    It's coming already.

by Dr Dana

IF YOU'RE A POLICYMAKER

If you're a policymaker,
    oh wise one in suits,
    Stop popping in schools
    just to pose in your boots.
Don't wander the halls
    with a photo-op grin,
    Then leave without seeing
    the mess we're in.
You tour our classrooms
    for all of five minutes,
    Then tweet "Teachers are heroes!"
    without stepping in it.
You miss the shortages,
    subs, books, and chairs,
    The unpaid overtime
    nobody shares.
We don't need your tweets
    or your ribbon-cut cheer,
    We need paper and pencils
    that magically appear.
We need time for planning,
    and lunches not rushed,
    Not "Wellness Week" slogans
    with fruit water hushed.
Come teach with no subs,
    no budget, no break,
    With thirty-eight kids
    and a copier ache.
Stand in my shoes
    when the Wi-Fi drops dead,
    While five different meetings
    fight for my head.
Sit through a day
    where your lunch is a race,
    And your "free period" vanishes
    without a trace.
Then draft your "reform"
    with a confident grin,
    And blame the collapse
    on the folks trapped within.

We've had "grit" campaigns
    and "growth mindset" drills,
    And yoga in gyms
    while ignoring the bills.
We've had trauma-informed meetings
    and "restorative" chats,
    While teachers buy paper
    from Target: imagine that.

YOUR STORY

I know I've only just started telling my story, but you needed to know what's really going on.

We are not alone. Okay — maybe we're alone every day for 10 hours in a room full of "students." But let's be honest: they're not friends, they're not colleagues, and they're definitely not people we can vent to about how broken the system is. They're kids. Our job is to show up for them, even while no one shows up for us.

So yes, teaching often feels like spending hours isolated in chaos — surrounded, but somehow still alone. That's why this chapter isn't about me anymore — it's about you. The next pages are for your story:

- The rants you wanted to scream in a staff meeting but didn't.

- The survival hacks you've invented out of sheer desperation.

- The dreams of what school could be if it weren't run on burnout.

You can scribble, doodle, confess, roast, or just stare at the blank page — whatever helps you breathe. If you'd rather scan or upload, there's a QR code waiting.

I won't promise your words will end up in my next book.
  But I also won't promise they won't. PLUS I'll only judge your handwriting a little.

Because here's the truth: Other jobs: shut up, show up, perform, cash the check.

In teaching it is: shut up, show up, perform, repeat until burnout — then start all over on Monday.

So go ahead. Use the next pages. They're yours now.

Scan here to submit your brilliance, sarcasm, or rage anonymously (or not).

www.hallpasspress.com

"Unless someone like you cares a whole awful lot, nothing is going to get better. It's not."

— The Lorax

"What is one ridiculous-but-real way you could make a teacher's day easier?"

"It takes a village… and maybe a functioning copier."
— Misquoted proverb, but Dr. Dana fixed for accuracy

If teachers had their own Lorax, what would it shout at the school board or admin or parents?

"Support teachers the way you support your Wi-Fi. Immediately. And with panic when it goes down."

— Unknown but True

Design the most wildly inappropriate Teacher Appreciation Week gift you can think of. (Corporate jet? A district-paid therapist? Or just soap in the staff bathroom?)

"You can't pour from an empty cup... unless you're a teacher, then they will hand you a broken cup and still expect a refill."

— Dr. Dana Lebental

If you could donate one magical object to every teacher's classroom, what would it be? (Yes, you can say wine.) Or "If you had $20 to spend on teacher morale, how would you use it (besides pizza)?"

"Those who can, teach. Those who can't, schedule another meeting about it."

— Misapplied wisdom

What's one kind of training that would actually be worth a teacher's time? Or if your district's PD had a Yelp review, what's the headline? (Examples: "Five hours of my life I'll never get back.")

"Do not judge me by my success, judge me by how many times I fell and got back up again."

— Nelson Mandela

If teachers had a mythical staff-lounge vending machine, what absurd-but-accurate items would it spit out? (Options might include: "5 free minutes of silence," "a working pen," or "copier toner blessed by a priest.")

"Life is what happens when you're busy making other plans."
— John Lennon

What's the one thing you'd fix first in education — and what's the "band-aid solution" they'll probably give instead?

"Be the change you wish to see in the world."

— Gandhi

If Gandhi taught middle school, what would make him quit by October? (I couldn't resist)

"I always wanted to be somebody, but now I realize I should have been more specific."

— Jane Wagner

"List 3 things that would keep teachers in the profession longer than succulents and Starbucks cards."

"Nothing says self-care like grading papers in a bubble bath."
— Dr. Dana Lebental

What is one practical, low-cost way the community could step in to make teachers' lives easier? When are you going to do this?

Other thoughts...

ACKNOWLEDGEMENTS

This book was born from both frustration and hope. Frustration at a system that too often undervalues, underpays, and overlooks the very people who hold the future of our children in their hands. And hope that by telling these stories, sharing these struggles, and shining a light on the realities of teaching, change might one day be possible.

First, I want to acknowledge my fellow teachers—the warriors of the classroom. You show up every day, even when the odds are stacked against you, even when exhaustion sets in, and even when appreciation feels scarce. You give pieces of yourselves in ways most people will never fully understand.

To the students, past and present, who have been the reason I walked into the classroom each morning: you are the "why" behind every late night, every creative lesson, and every extra ounce of patience. You taught me as much as I ever taught you.

To the families and friends who listened to my venting, dried my tears, celebrated small victories, and reminded me that I am more than my job: thank you for grounding me.

And to the readers who may not be teachers but who care enough to pick up this book: may these words open your eyes to both the struggles and the extraordinary dedication within this profession. May you carry forward the message that teachers deserve not just recognition, but true respect and systemic change.

Finally, to every teacher on the brink of burnout who wonders if anyone notices or cares: I see you, I hear you, and I hope this book helped you feel a little less alone.

www.hallpasspress.com

ABOUT THE AUTHOR

Dr. Dana Lebental, Ed.D. has been orbiting (and occasionally escaping) public education for over 21 years. Fourteen of those years were spent in the trenches as a teacher, department chair, and assistant principal. The rest? Spent taking much-needed breaks, only to return—because, despite every attempt to walk away, education keeps pulling her back.

She holds a Doctorate in Education and an MBA, and has had more classroom trauma than any one person should have to explain at brunch. Dana has taught everything from Biology to burnout survival, conducted labs with one working faucet, and has been told to "smile more" during staff meetings held on her lunch break.

This book is the result of loving a profession that doesn't love you back, and still showing up. She now splits her time between advocating for educational sanity, helping international artists navigate the U.S. immigration system, and offering brutally honest advice with a side of sarcasm.

Dana Lebental is a keynote speaker and professional magician who makes problems—and boredom—disappear faster than your budget. Forget canned speeches and corporate buzzwords; she delivers sarcasm, sleight of hand, and the kind of truth bombs HR would rather you not hear.

She doesn't "give a talk." She hijacks the stage, makes the audience laugh, squirm, and think—and somehow leaves them wanting more. It's not motivation, it's magic with a side of reality check.

Where keynote meets magic—messages that stick, moments you'll never forget (and possibly never recover from).

Connect with Dana at linkedin.com —or better yet, hire her for your next event. Just don't expect her to pull a rabbit out of a hat; she's too busy pulling the curtain back on nonsense.